Special Themes for Moving & Learning

Rae Pica
Creator/Director of Moving & Learning
Rochester, New Hampshire

Human Kinetics Books
Champaign, Illinois

Library of Congress Cataloging-in-Publication Data

Pica, Rae, 1953-
    Special themes for moving & learning / Rae Pica.
        p.   cm.
    ISBN 0-87322-319-5
    1. Movement education.   I. Title.   II. Title: Special themes for
    moving and learning.
    GV452.P525   1991
    372.86--dc20   90-27862
                                                                        CIP

ISBN: 0-87322-319-5

Developmental Editor: Judy Patterson Wright, PhD
Assistant Editors: Dawn Levy and Kari Nelson
Copyeditor: Molly Bentsen
Proofreader: Karin Leszczynski
Production Director: Ernie Noa
Typesetter: Brad Colson and Kathy Boudreau-Fuoss
Text Design: Keith Blomberg
Text Layout: Tara Welsch
Cover Design: Dawn Bates
Cover Illustration: Dawn Bates
Interior Illustrations: Dawn Bates
Interior Photo: Jack Adams
Printer: Versa Press

Human Kinetics books are available at special discounts for bulk purchase for sales promotions, premiums, fundraising, or educational use. Special editions or book excerpts can also be created to specification. For details, contact the Special Sales Manager at Human Kinetics.

Printed in the United States of America

10 9 8 7 6 5 4 3 2 1

Human Kinetics Books
A Division of Human Kinetics Publishers, Inc.
Box 5076, Champaign, IL 61825-5076
1-800-747-4457

Canada Office:
Human Kinetics Publishers, Inc.
P.O. Box 2503, Windsor, ON N8Y 4S2
1-800-465-7301 (in Canada only)

UK Office:
Human Kinetics Publishers (UK) Ltd.
P.O. Box 18
Rawdon, Leeds LS19 6TG
England
(0532) 504211

This book is dedicated to the memory of New Hampshire's "Teacher in Space," Christa McAuliffe, and to the "explorer" in teachers everywhere.

Welcome to the Moving & Learning Series

Written by Rae Pica
with music by Richard Gardzina

"An important and much-needed contribution to the movement education of young children. Practical, well written, and developmentally appropriate. Rae Pica has done a masterful job, and Richard Gardzina is to be congratulated for his many fine contributions."
David L. Gallahue
Professor, Indiana University

What is the Moving & Learning Series?

- A year's worth of activities *and* music at your fingertips!
- Programs that require minimal planning and preparation and make your job easier.
- Themes and activities that fit easily into your present curriculum.
- Activities and music that kids will love.
- Programs that are developmentally appropriate for children of all ages.

This is the *only* series of its kind for day-care, preschool, and pre-K staff and early childhood and elementary professionals. Only the Moving & Learning Series helps you to develop motor skills, concepts, and rhythm in young children by combining music with movement activities.

Whether you're searching for an activity program for your toddler, preschool, or pre-K through third-grade class or for innovative music to motivate your kids, the Moving & Learning Series is the answer to your needs.

- Easy and convenient to use, *Toddlers Moving & Learning* (Second Edition) is a complete program featuring 33 lessons and 99 activities—and three audiocassettes of original music. It's great for children ages 18 to 36 months.

- *Preschoolers Moving & Learning* (Second Edition) is for children ages 3 to 5 years. It comes complete with five audiocassettes and 40 lessons with 200 activities—enough for a whole school year!

- Reduce your teaching preparation time with *Early Elementary Children Moving & Learning*. Geared to 5- to 9-year-olds, this program includes five audiocassettes and 40 lesson plans with 200 movement activities. Spend your time teaching and let the Moving & Learning Series do the class preparation for you.

- Need additional music for your activity program? *More Music for Moving & Learning* (Second Edition) comes with six cassettes and features 62 songs and five of your favorite themes, including animals, holidays, relaxation, exploring different cultures, and role-playing. It's designed for toddlers, preschoolers, and children ages 5 to 9 years.

- *Let's Move & Learn* (Second Edition) is a two-cassette package of 32 movement-motivating songs for parents to use with their toddlers, preschoolers, and kindergartners through third graders.

- *Special Themes for Moving & Learning*, appropriate for children ages 4 to 8, enables you to teach 38 popular classroom themes through 190 movement activities.

For more information on the Moving & Learning Series, please call Human Kinetics Publishers TOLL FREE at 1-800-747-4457, or write P.O. Box 5076, Champaign, IL 61825-5076.

CONTENTS

PREFACE

Study units, or classroom themes, are a common part of early childhood and elementary education. They help to break up the year, to focus the children's attention on a particular subject, and to heighten their enthusiasm for it. Probably hundreds of "circle time" and activity books based on such themes have been written for preschool, kindergarten, and primary-grade teachers. These books offer suggestions for exploring each topic through field trips, games, recipes, stories, and sometimes creative movement.

But what of the teacher or parent who believes especially in children's learning through movement, so that abstract concepts can become more concrete? She or he has to wade through all of those recipes and stories to find a few movement activities. The same applies for the movement or physical education specialist who has lots of movement activities to choose from but would like to offer some with a common concept—perhaps to coincide with what's being taught in the classroom. To my knowledge, no book exists that explores concepts through movement alone. So I decided to write one!

Movement is an important element in programs for young children. It enhances psycho-motor development, and it contributes to the development of a positive self-image, self-confidence, creativity, and self-expression. Movement also stimulates the learning process. There is increasing evidence that because a child's earliest learning is based on motor development, subsequent learning is, too. And abstract concepts can become concrete, forming long-lasting impressions, when they are physically experienced. As Confucius said, "What I hear, I forget. What I see, I remember. What I do, I know."

Therefore, if a topic is to make a true impression on children—if they are going to really know the subject—they must experience it, certainly among other ways, through movement.

Unfortunately, movement education is an intimidating subject to some teachers. They feel they don't know enough about movement to do it justice—that they should be experts before making movement part of the curriculum. And with all other subjects teachers have to deal with, the idea of becoming a movement expert can seem insurmountable. Unfortunately, too, even after attending workshops or reading books on the topic, teachers quite often come away with theory only. And if there's one thing of which I'm certain, it's that teachers have little time for converting theory into practice.

Even teachers who are fairly comfortable with movement can feel overwhelmed by the idea of creating, searching for, and accumulating enough movement activities to use. And once accumulated, the activities still have to be sorted through and arranged to make some sort of sense. Whether an arrangement is done by skill progression or by concept, the teacher can plan on investing a great deal of time.

All of that is why the Moving & Learning Series was developed—to provide accessible, practical movement activities and ideas for teachers and parents of young children, easily usable whether or not they have experience in movement education. And as part of the series, *Special Themes for Moving & Learning* provides usable activities that happen to be grouped according to study units.

Special Themes for Moving & Learning is the sixth project in the Moving & Learning Series. It is written for teachers and parents of children ages 4 to 8 (preschool through second grade). It is for those teachers and parents who want their children to discover—to physically experience concepts and to do so creatively. It's for those who sometimes do movement and those who regularly do movement—and even those who've never done movement! It's for everyone looking for an infusion of new ideas.

I'd like to offer acknowledgement and thanks to my illustrator and friend, Dawn Bates, who has once more transformed an ordinary book into a magical one. Special thanks to Rainer Martens, Judy Patterson Wright, Kathy Read, Rick Hollwedel, Scott Wikgren, and the entire Human Kinetics staff for their dedication to the Moving & Learning Series. Thanks, too, to Johanna Booth-Miner for her helpful comments, and to my friend Sue Robinson, whose enthusiasm and support helped keep me going throughout this project. Finally, thanks to my husband, Richard Gardzina. He may not have contributed his wonderful music to this book, but he contributes in many ways to everything I write.

HOW TO USE THIS BOOK

I have carefully selected the 38 themes in this book, based on my study of a number of other activity books as well as discussions with many early childhood and elementary teaching professionals. I believe the topics are among the most popular of classroom themes, and all lend themselves to movement exploration.

For every theme, there are five principal activities, which gives you 190 activities to select from—a full year's worth! Although the holidays and seasons appear in the book in their order in the school year, the activities themselves are not arranged in any particular order. You may choose to use some or all of the five activities at one time, perhaps as part of a 30- or 45-minute movement session. Or you can use one activity per day, making movement a daily part of your study of a unit.

Some of the activities involve nonlocomotor skills (or movements requiring little space) and therefore lend themselves easily to circle time. Others suggest variations intended to promote further study or to provide extra ideas for future use. A few of the activities require a bit of advance planning in the way of choosing a piece of music or putting words or pictures on scraps of paper that the children will draw from a hat or box. And some of the activities can be completed in just a few minutes, while others may require more time or several repetitions before they can be accomplished successfully.

My suggestion is that you familiarize yourself with the variety of themes offered in *Special Themes for Moving & Learning* before putting this book to use. Or, if you simply select in advance the activity or activities you want to explore with the children, you can ensure there won't be any last-minute glitches. For example, if you happen to be studying occupations one week and you want to concentrate on homemaking, you can see from the table of contents that that topic is covered in the theme called ''Keeping House'' in chapter 8. The next step is to determine how many activities you want to perform on a particular day. If you know on Monday that you'll have time for only one activity on Tuesday, you should decide which of the five activities it'll be. And if you choose the activity called A Dusting Dance, by reading its description you'll see that you need some pieces of cloth for the children to use.

I realize that, developmentally speaking, there is quite a range of skill levels and problem-solving abilities among 4- to 8-year-olds. But, as you know, each child develops at her or his own rate. Therefore, not only can you expect a range of responses from children of varying ages, but you may also find children of the same age responding to the book's challenges in different ways. That's okay; it's what movement exploration is all about.

As the teacher, however, you are responsible to know when children need more help than what I have suggested with the activities. For instance, if some of your children can't yet read and an activity calls for words to be drawn from a container, you may choose to put pictures or colors instead on the paper scraps—or you can plan to read the words for the children. You may also find that with some activities you have to provide more verbal assistance for some groups of children. For example, in the activity called The Bank Teller (under the theme ''More Professions'' in chapter 8), different dollar amounts are represented by different locomotor skills. If some of your children have trouble remembering the correlations, there's no reason why you can't tell them. But no one knows your children better than you—so you're the only one who can accurately assess their particular needs.

As you can see by reviewing the table of contents, there is some overlapping of themes. *Animals* and *The Sea* are topics that certainly fall under the heading of "Nature" (chapter 5). But they are such broad topics that I've given them chapters of their own (chapters 6 and 7, respectively). Similarly, although there is a theme called "Nutrition" (in chapter 2, "Health Awareness"), there is a food activity under the theme "Thanksgiving" in chapter 4 (naturally!). There is also a squirrel (animal) activity under the "Autumn" theme (chapter 3) and a feelings activity under the "Valentine's Day" theme (chapter 4) as well as a theme devoted to feelings in the chapter on self-awareness (chapter 1).

For some activities I suggest the use of recorded music—because music tends to inspire movement, and it can make movement even more fun for the children. This is the first project in the Moving & Learning Series, though, to be produced without accompanying music. Because children need to experience movement on its own, *Special Themes for Moving & Learning* relies more on the use of imagery and the movement elements of space, shape, force, flow, time, and rhythm (both the children's personal rhythms and the rhythms of words).

For the most part, there's very little work involved for you in using this book. A number of teachers have told me how difficult it is to implement some movement programs due to the materials and equipment required. So I've purposely created activities calling for no or few props. And those props that are required are items found in a typical classroom.

In essence, all that will be required of you—in addition to a bit of advance preparation—is the presentation of the challenges suggested for each activity. Oh, sometimes you might have to read a poem aloud or sing with the children (all of the songs are sung to the tunes of old classics, so you're sure to know the melodies). To help you locate these, I've placed quotation marks around the titles of those activities that contain either poems or song lyrics. But, generally speaking, I've already done the hard part, and it's left to you and the children to do the fun part: the exploration!

I do hope that you'll enjoy the activities in this book as much as children do—because I firmly believe that, whatever our age, we should never stop moving and learning!

As always, I welcome your questions and comments. So don't hesitate to contact me through Human Kinetics Publishers.

chapter 1

Self-Awareness

body parts
the senses
feelings

Self-Awareness

BODY PARTS

LEARNING OBJECTIVES: To enhance body image and perceptual-motor development.

Show Me

Background Information. The traditional game Simon Says can be a wonderful body parts identification activity, except for the fact that its rules eliminate children—and those who need to participate the most are usually the first to go! Show Me is simply Simon Says without elimination. (If some children respond incorrectly, you can always enthusiastically point out some of the other children's responses so those in error have a chance to adjust accordingly.)

Activity. Explain to the children that this game is like Simon Says, but you're going to say "Show me" instead. And no one will have to quit playing the game!
  You can ask the children to show you how they do the following:

Touch toes	Pucker mouths
Blink eyes	Put hands on hips
Cover ears	Touch shoulders
Bend knees	Squeeze elbows
Stand on one foot	Pat tummies
Nod heads	Wave hands
Wiggle fingers	Give themselves a hug!
Wiggle noses	

Mirror Game

Background Information. This game is similar to Show Me, except that you'll be giving the children visual cues instead of verbal ones. Verbal cues enhance listening skills; the Mirror Game has children physically imitate what they're seeing, developing visual awareness.
  Talk to the children about mirrors and how they reflect images. Where in their homes do they have mirrors? What kinds of activities might they perform while looking in a mirror?

Activity. Stand facing the children, in a spot where they all have a clear view of you. Ask them to imagine that you're looking into a mirror and that they are your reflection. That means they must do exactly what they see you do.
  Silently perform many of the same movements from Show Me. As most of these are static poses or simple movements, the children will soon have the knack. (Move slowly when changing from one position to the next!)

Alternate Activity.   For more challenge, perform movements such as hopping or jumping in place (or from side to side), waving arms, shaking the body or various body parts, and so on.

My Face Can Say . . .

Background Information.   Talk to the children about body language and how sometimes we can express what we're feeling or what we want to say with no words at all. And the face, being the most expressive body part we have, is very capable of doing just that!

Activity.   Ask children to show you, with their faces only, how they would express the following:

"I'm tired."   "I'm sad."

"I'm mad."   "That smells good."

"I'm afraid."   "That smells awful."

"That tastes yummy."   "What a surprise!"

"That tastes yucky."   "I'm happy!"

My Hands Can Say . . .

Background Information.   Explain that, like our faces, our hands can also "say" many things for us. You might use this opportunity to discuss sign language.

Activity.   Ask the children to show you, with their hands only, how they would express the following:

"Hello."   "Stop!"

"Come here."   "I'm mad."

"Go away."   "I'm cold."

"Naughty, naughty."   "Goodbye!"

"I'm hot."   "Yea!"

"I'm scared."

"The Body Poem"

Background Information.   Read the following poem to the children without any activity at first, so they know what to expect. Besides the parts mentioned in the poem, what other body parts do they have more than one of? How many of each? How many teeth and hairs do they think they have?

Activity.   Explain to the children that you're going to read "The Body Poem" again, and this time they should touch or display the appropriate body parts as they're mentioned in the poem. For the last segment, they should shrug on "So why, do you suppose" and move their hands, from top to bottom, the length of their bodies on the next two lines.
   The poem is as follows:

> I have two feet,
> Two ears, two legs,
> Ten fingers and ten toes;
>
> I have two knees,
> Two lips, two hands,
> And even two elbows;
>
> I have two eyes
> And four eyelids.
> So why, do you suppose,
>
> With all these parts
> On my body
> I only have one nose?!

Note. This activity should be performed slowly at first. But as the children become familiar with the poem (and are even reciting it themselves), they'll have lots of fun if you do it faster each time. Once they're thoroughly familiar with it, you might want to introduce them to the concept of *accelerando*, beginning the poem very slowly and gradually speaking faster and faster as you recite the lines—so it actually ends in a rush!

THE SENSES

LEARNING OBJECTIVES: To inspire children to consider the five senses and to foster appreciation for their functions.

Tasting

Background Information.   Talk to the children about their favorite foods and the way they taste. How do those tastes make them feel? What tastes don't they like? Why? Discuss the tastes mentioned here, asking the children to describe how each makes them feel.

Activity.   Now that you've talked about how various tastes make them feel, the children are going to show you, with their faces only, how these tastes make them feel:

A sour lemon	Hot chocolate
A very bubbly drink	A pickle
Salty potato chips	Peanut butter
Spicy food (e.g., a hot pepper)	Ice cream (their favorite flavor)

Smelling

Background Information.   Like tasting, smelling different things can create a variety of reactions in us. Talk to the children about how the various odors listed here make them feel. What are their favorite smells? Why?

Activity.   This activity is similar to Tasting; this time the children will show you with their whole bodies (or the appropriate parts) how certain odors make them feel. Odors can include these:

Sour milk	A clean, crisp day
Cookies baking	Onions
A skunk	A rose (or other flowers)

Hearing

Background Information.   Talk to the children about all the various sounds they might hear during the course of a day. Do they hear different sounds at home than they do at school? What sounds are pleasing to them? Which do they find unpleasant? Why?

Activity.   For this exercise, you'll have to plan ahead a bit to gather a variety of noisemakers. Ask the children to move in the way each sound (which you create with the noisemakers) makes them feel like moving. Try sounds like these:

> Pots and pans being struck
> A bell
> Clapping
> A whistle
> A foot stamping
> A coffee can partially filled with sand and shaken
> Velcro tabs being separated
> A glass lightly struck with a spoon

Alternate Activity.   In lieu of noisemakers, you can use only body sounds. In addition to clapping and stamping, you might whistle, click your tongue, snap your fingers, smack your lips, ''drum'' a thigh, or inhale and exhale loudly.

Touching

Background Information.   Touch is probably the sense we take most for granted. A smell or a sound can draw our full attention and even invoke memories of times gone by. A beautiful sight (or a startling one) causes us to pause and take notice and forms a lasting impression in the mind. And tasting often provides some of our most pleasurable daily sensations. But things we touch (unless we are consciously stroking a cat's fur,

for instance, or are burned by a hot stove) usually make less of an impression. We pick up a toothbrush without noticing the smoothness of the handle. We put on our clothes without registering the feel of the cloth. We close a door without really feeling the shape and texture of the doorknob.

Talk to the children about such daily events, asking them to describe the feel of some of the objects they commonly touch. Mention items of varying textures, like a glass, a ''scratchy'' sweater, warm water, or a pencil. Then ask the children to look around the room and point out some of the different textures they find.

Activity. Ahead of time, choose two pieces of music, one soft and slow, the other upbeat. Play one and ask the children to move, or dance, around the room, patting and stroking lots of different textures. Do the things they touch make them feel like moving in different ways? Now put on the second piece of music, asking the children to perform the ''touching dance'' again. Does the style of the music inspire them to touch things in different ways? Finally, briefly repeat the activity without any music at all. How does this affect the children's responses?

Seeing

Background Information. What are the most beautiful sights the children have ever seen? What do they see when they first open their eyes in the morning? What are their favorite colors? Why? What faraway place would they like to see someday? These are the kinds of questions you can ask the children to get them thinking about the sense of sight.

Activity. With this exercise, the children are going to consider sight by experiencing its opposite—sightlessness. Explain to them that, now that they've talked about seeing lots of things, they're going to discover what it's like to do some things without seeing.

Begin by asking the children to each sit in their own personal space. Then instruct them to close their eyes. Do they feel any different? (These questions don't necessarily require a verbal response from the children; rather, they're asked to cause the children to consider what they're experiencing.) Have them briefly open their eyes (to reorient themselves) and then close their eyes again and stand up, keeping eyes closed. Once standing, the children should open their eyes for a moment (they should always do this momentarily between activities), and then close them again. Does standing with eyes closed feel different?

Continue this process, cueing the children to experience the differences with eyes open and then closed in doing the following:

Stand on tiptoe

Stand (flat-footed) on one foot

Stand (briefly) on one foot on tiptoe

Stand flat-footed and lean, alternately, in all four directions; repeat on tiptoe

Take a few steps forward; backward; to either side

FEELINGS

LEARNING OBJECTIVES: To cause the children to consider and accept their feelings; to promote self-expression.

Feeling Sad

Background Information. Discuss sadness with the children, asking for examples of times they've felt sad. How did their faces and bodies look when they were feeling sad? How did they move? Did they move quickly or slowly? "Bouncy" or "dragging"? Assure the children that it's okay to feel sad sometimes—everybody does.

Activity. Put on a soft, slow (and, if possible, *sad*) piece of music for this activity. (Samuel Barber's *Adagio for Strings* is a perfect example, but there are many instrumental numbers —often found on recordings used for quiet times—that would also be appropriate.) As the music is playing, ask the children to show you how their faces look when they're sad. Continue with the following questions:

How do you walk when you're sad?

How could you show me with your hands and arms that you're sad?

Can you make up a "sad dance" to this music?

Can you show me you're sad in a sitting position? Lying down?

"Feeling Mad"

Background Information. Anger is an emotion all children are familiar with, and they need to be assured that it's legitimate. It's okay to feel mad, as long as they don't hurt themselves or someone else. Also, anger—like other emotions—requires expression. What are some of the ways people might express their anger? Which ways are "positive" and which "negative"? In your discussion, be sure to mention those forms of expression found in the poem here.

Activity. Ask the children to act out the lines of this poem:

> I clench my fists
> And raise them high,
> I stomp my feet real loud.
> I walk around with shoulders hunched;
> My face, it has a scowl.
>
> I kick the floor
> And scuff my feet,
> I'm acting really "bad";
> But I can't help the way I feel
> Because, you see, I'm mad!

Feeling Fear

Background Information.   Fear is one emotion many people—young and old—don't like to admit to. But, like any other emotion, it's perfectly legitimate at times. What are some times when we might feel afraid?

Activity.   Ask the children to imagine this scene: It's Halloween night and they're in a haunted house. The house is very dark, there are cobwebs everywhere, and the floorboards are creaking.
  Now ask the following questions:

How does your face look?

How do your hands show that you're afraid?

How do you walk? Run?

If you were standing still and trying to hide in a corner, how would your body look?

What might you do to stop being afraid? Show me.

Show Me What You're Feeling

Background Information.   Talk to the children about all the feelings covered in the activity described, particularly those they've yet to experience through movement. Discuss the fact that there are really only two ways to express emotions: with words and with the body.

Activity.   Explain to the children that you're going to express or create an emotion with words, or verbally. They, in turn, will demonstrate through their facial expressions and body positions how your words make them feel. (Remember that the way you use your voice will be very important in conveying the appropriate emotion.)
  You might include the following:

"What a surprise!"

"Ouch!"

"Goody, goody!"

"Oh no—what am I going to do?"

"That's yucky!"

"I don't have anyone to play with."

"I'm so proud of myself!"

"Boo!"

"I love you!"

Alternate Activity.   You can later try the same activity with the children moving. Have them begin walking around the room. Present one of the verbal expressions, and have children respond by moving (or simply walking) in the way that the words make them feel. Allow time for them to express the emotion, and then present the next. But vary the length of time between emotions so the children don't know when to expect the next.

Feeling Calm/Feeling Nervous

Background Information.   Naturally, you can only expect your children to respond to those emotions with which they've had experience. For example, it's unlikely they would be able to depict such "adult" emotions as *disillusionment* or *anxiety*. But *calm* and *nervous*, although more of a challenge than the emotions in previous activities, are feelings the children can relate to if you spend some time discussing them.

Calm, for instance, is a very relaxed feeling—like that experienced just before falling asleep at night. At those times, muscles feel loose and "liquid." Images that can help describe relaxation include feeling like a rag doll, a limp noodle, or a wet washcloth. Other times when children might have experienced calmness include while sitting by a lake, observing a bird soar through the sky, or watching the sun set.

What are some times when the children have felt nervous? Nervous is sort of a combination of scared and worried. Have they ever worried that it might rain on the day of a big outing? Have they ever lost sight of parents in a big store and felt nervous until spotting them again? How did their muscles and bodies feel at those times? Were they loose or tense? Ask them to show you.

Activity. The children are going to experience the differences between feeling calm and feeling nervous at various levels in space. They begin at a standing level. When you say the word *calm*, the children should make their bodies as relaxed as possible. When you say *nervous*, they tense up. (Vary the time between verbal cues. Also, remember that the quality of your voice is very important; it should sound like the word you're saying.) Repeat this process with the children kneeling, sitting, and, finally, lying down.

Note. This is an excellent relaxation technique in any context. Learning to create ''calmness'' in the body is a wonderful tool in controlling tension. And there are those who believe that tension control can help children learn better.

chapter

2

HEALTH AWARENESS

nutrition
hygiene
bodies
in
motion

NUTRITION

LEARNING OBJECTIVES: To acquaint children with the five basic food groups; to encourage the children to eat well.

Fruit, Glorious Fruit

Background Information. Fruit is one of the five basic food groups (the others being bread products, dairy products, vegetables, and proteins). Fruits provide us with lots of vitamins and minerals and are fun to eat. But fruit is also special in that you can make so many things to eat and drink with different kinds.

What are the favorite fruits of the children in your group? Can they name some of the foods and drinks that are made with them?

Activity. Ask the children to show you the following:

Oranges

An orange being peeled
An orange section
Orange sherbet being scooped
Orange juice being poured

Apples

An apple hanging from a tree
An apple slice
An apple pie
Applesauce simmering on the stove

Bananas

A banana being peeled
A loaf of banana bread
A banana muffin
A banana slice floating in cereal and milk

Grapes

A bunch of grapes hanging on a vine
Grape jelly being spread
A raisin
A slice of raisin toast

Note. The children can either pretend to _be_ or _do_ these activities and items, depending upon their interpretations. For example, some might show you what it's like to pour the orange juice, while others show you what it's like to be the orange juice being poured.

Also, you may want to discuss the relationship between grapes and raisins.

In the Beginning

Background Information.   Where does bread come from? Why, the supermarket, of course—although some "enlightened" children might say the bakery. But back in the "olden days," children knew where bread really came from: Their mothers made it from flour and water and yeast, and it filled the house with a most wonderful aroma.

Talk to the children about this basic food, explaining that it does not originate on the grocer's shelves. Describe the process of mixing flour and water and yeast into dough, kneading the dough, letting it rise, rolling it out with a rolling pin, shaping it to fit a bread pan, and baking it.

Activity.   Tell the children you're going to be the baker and they're going to be the ingredients. And when you're through with them, they're going to be loaves of bread all ready to eat.

Use the appropriate hand and arm movements for each step of the process, as you pretend to do to the children the steps listed. They, in turn, will pretend to have the following _done_ to them. The process is as follows:

Stir the flour and water and yeast together.
Knead the dough.
Cover the dough with a cloth and let it rise.
Punch the dough down.
Roll the dough out.
Shape the dough into a loaf.
Let the dough rise again.
Bake the dough—it rises even more and becomes firm.
Remove bread from the pan.
Slice the bread and eat it!

Alternate Activity.   Ask the children to take on the shapes of other types of dough, including the following:

A pretzel   A gingerbread man
A muffin   A round loaf

"From Cow to Cone"

Background Information.   Dairy products as a food group are an important source of calcium, which helps keep our bones and teeth strong. The most common dairy product for most children is milk, but their favorite is probably ice cream.

Although the process described here is not strictly correct, it will give the children an idea of the process involved in creating ice cream from milk and of the relationship among several dairy products. Talk to the children about the process, explaining that after the cow is milked, the cream rises to the top and is skimmed off. The cream is then churned into butter, which can then be made into ice cream by stirring it as it freezes. (Ice cream is most often made from cream but can also be made from butterfat.)

Activity. The following song is sung to the tune of "The Farmer in the Dell." Decide on movements to go along with the verses (I've included some possibilities), and sing it with the children:

> The farmer milks the cow (milking action with hands and arms),
> The farmer milks the cow,
> Hi-ho-the-dairy-o,
> The farmer milks the cow.
>
> **Second verse**: The farmer skims the cream (a skimming motion, as though with a ladle in hand).
>
> **Third verse**: The farmer churns the cream (an up-and-down motion with one hand above the other, as though holding a broom handle).
>
> **Fourth verse**: The farmer stirs the butter (stirring motion).
>
> **Fifth verse**: The butter turns to ice cream (pretending to be licking ice cream in a cone).
>
> **Sixth verse**: The ice cream slowly melts (pretending to be melting ice cream).

Veggies

Background Information. Vegetables are not known to be the favorite food group of most children. In fact, a cajoling "Eat your vegetables" is probably the most common line spoken to children at the dinner table.

This activity, which gives the children yet another opportunity to pretend to be inanimate objects, may help give them an awareness of some vegetables' origins and an appreciation for the work that goes into preparing them. Talk to the children about the vegetables and actions listed. Show pictures if you have them.

Activity. Ask the children to pretend to be the following:

> A carrot being pulled out of the ground
> A carrot in the blender (for carrot juice)
> A potato being washed
> A potato being mashed
> Lettuce being pulled apart

Lettuce being tossed in a salad
A pea pod
A pea rolling out of the pod

An ear of corn being shucked
An ear of corn being eaten

A Balanced Diet

Background Information.   Review the four food groups already explored, and talk about the fifth: proteins. The protein group can include fish and meats and products belonging in other food groups (for example, eggs, cheeses, beans, and peanut butter).

To have a healthy, balanced diet, people should eat a certain amount of food from each of the five basic groups every day.

On construction or poster paper, make lists of foods and drinks that fall under each of the food group categories. Or cut pictures from magazines and paste them under the headings.

Activity.   Divide your children into groups of five and instruct them to create, with their bodies, a well-balanced meal. This involves deciding who is to belong to which food group and then specifically which foods and drinks to be. Whatever foods and drinks the children choose, they should be recognizable. In other words, each child should find a way to look or move so that his or her choice can be guessed with a minimum of effort.

Give the children enough time to work all of this out. Then you have two choices: You can either move from group to group, acting as the guesser, or you can have one group at a time demonstrate, with the rest of the class guessing.

Alternate Activity.   If your class isn't large enough to divide into groups of five, have the children draw scraps of paper assigning each to a food group. You then act as "chef," creating one meal at a time by calling for a vegetable, a fruit, a dairy product, a bread product, and a protein. One child from each of these groups then comes to the center of the room (the "plate") and poses or moves like the food or drink of her or his choice. Then the guessing takes place.

HYGIENE

LEARNING OBJECTIVES: To call attention to the importance of good hygiene; to make hygiene seem like fun, so the subject will have a pleasant association.

"Washing Hands"

Background Information. One of the most important aspects of good hygiene is hand-washing. Children need to learn early that washing hands with soap and warm water eliminates germs and can help prevent colds and other illnesses from being spread. Germs, however, are a puzzling concept to young children. After all, they have no evidence that germs really exist!

Talk to the children about germs, explaining that some of the ways they're spread are through touching, sneezing, and coughing. That's why it's important, when someone has a cold, that he or she wash hands following each sneeze or cough.

Activity. Ask the children to stand in a circle and hold hands. Explain that they're going to go around in a circle while you chant a rhyme. But every time they hear the word *achoo*, they're to let go of each other's hands and pretend to wash their hands in the center of the circle (which they're imagining is a sink). They then re-join hands and continue to circle when you begin to chant again. The chant is as follows:

> I am a germ;
> I can be spread
> From you to you to you.
> All it takes is a cough or a sneeze—
> I'll get you with an *achoo!*

<u>Note</u>. Vary the tempo at which you recite the chant, saying it slowly or quickly at times, as well as at a moderate tempo.

"Hair Care"

Background Information. Chances are your children are not yet taking care of their own hair. So pretending to do so in the following activity should make them feel more "grown-up." Talk to them about all the things we can do to make sure we have clean, attractive-looking hair, stressing the fact that hair care is also a part of good hygiene.

Activity. The following song is performed to the tune of "Here We Go 'Round the Mulberry Bush." Familiarize the children with it so they can sing it with you as they act out the words. On the last verse, the children can pretend to admire themselves in a mirror. The song is as follows:

This is the way we wash our hair,
Wash our hair, wash our hair.
This is the way we wash our hair
So early in the morning.

Second verse: Rinse our hair

Third verse: Towel dry

Fourth verse: Blow it dry

Fifth verse: Comb our hair

Sixth verse: Look so nice

"Rub-a-Dub-Dub"

Background Information. Talk to the children about bathing. What do they like best about it? Does the water feel good? Do they like the slipperiness of the soap? Does scrubbing with a washcloth make their skin feel tingly?

Activity. In addition to being an exercise in hygiene, the following poem is great for body parts identification. The children act out the lines accordingly, pretending to wash the body parts mentioned.

Rub-a-dub-dub,
I sit in my tub
Washing my face and ears.
My face will shine;
It'll look so fine
And I'll be able to hear!

Rub-a-dub-dub,
I sit in my tub
Washing my hands and arms.
They'll be so clean
They'll practically gleam
And I will feel like a charm!

Rub-a-dub-dub,
I sit in my tub
Washing my back and tummy.
My body will glow
From head to toe—
I am going to look yummy!

Rub-a-dub-dub,
I sit in my tub
Washing my legs and feet.
I'll make them shine
Because they're mine;
Being clean is such a treat!

Brushing Teeth

Background Information.   Talk to the children about the importance of brushing teeth, discussing problems like tooth decay and gum disease. How many times a day do they brush their teeth? What kind of toothpaste do they use? What color toothbrush do they have?

Activity.   The children are going to pretend to be various things involved with brushing teeth. Instruct them to think carefully about each of the following before showing you what they look like. Ask the children to pretend to be these items:

A tube of toothpaste
A tube of toothpaste being rolled up from the bottom
A tube of toothpaste that's been squished all over
Toothpaste being squeezed from the tube
The shape of a toothbrush
A toothbrush in motion
A battery-powered toothbrush

Caring for Our Clothes

Background Information.   Clean clothes are nearly as important as a clean body to put them on. What are some of the ways we can take care of our clothes? Possible responses include washing, ironing, folding, and hanging them properly.

Activity. Ask the children to choose an item of clothing they'd like to be (e.g., a pair of pants, a shirt, a skirt). They then take on the shape of that piece of clothing and show you what it would look like when the following things are being done to it:

Washed in a washing machine
Washed and wrung by hand
Tumble-dried
Dried on a clothesline in the breeze
Ironed
Hung on a hanger
Folded and placed in a drawer

BODIES IN MOTION

LEARNING OBJECTIVES: To enhance bodily and spatial awareness; to strengthen imaginations; to practice locomotor and nonlocomotor skills.

Follow the Leader

Background Information. This activity serves three purposes: It provides practice in various locomotor and nonlocomotor skills; it offers an opportunity for the children to physically imitate what they're seeing; and it serves as a review of various movement elements. *Locomotor* is movement that transports the body from one place to another while *nonlocomotor* movement occurs as the body remains in place. Before beginning, simply explain to the children that you're going to lead them around the room, moving in a variety of ways, and that they should try to look and move as much like you as possible.

Activity. Lead your children around the room, performing any locomotor skills that they've had practice with and pausing occasionally to perform a nonlocomotor skill (e.g., shaking, bending, stretching, twisting). Be sure to alter the force (heavy/light) and time (slow/fast) of your movements and to incorporate a variety of shapes. Possible shapes include large, small, wide, narrow, and crooked.

How Many Parts?

Background Information. Nonlocomotor movements are performed with the body remaining in one spot. All can be executed with the body as a whole, but there are also a number of body parts that can execute these skills. Explain this to the children, perhaps choosing one nonlocomotor skill from the list here and demonstrating.

Activity. First ask the children to show you how the *whole body* performs each skill in the list. Then ask them to find out how many body *parts* can also perform them. Allow enough time for the children to amply experiment with each skill. The nonlocomotor skills can include these:

Shaking   Twisting
Bending   Swinging
Stretching   Falling

"A Walking Trip"

Background Information. Explain to the children that they're going to go on an imaginary walking trip, through many different environments. Then talk specifically about what it would be like to walk through the various environments mentioned in the following poem. Also, discuss any terms that may require explanation, like *briskly*, and *waning*.

Activity. Read the poem, with the children pretending to walk as described.

Briskly we start out
On a bright sunny day;
We have lots of energy
To get us on our way!

Up a steep, steep hill,
Then down the other side;
Once again on flatter ground
We can lengthen our stride.

We pause at the curb
Looking left, looking right,
Waiting 'til it's safe to cross
Between the lines of white.

Now through a meadow
With grass so tall and green
And across the slippery rocks
Of a swift shallow stream.

Into the forest,
It's almost dark as night
With thousands of leaves above
Keeping out the sunlight.

Tangles of branches,
Fallen trunks, roots, and rocks
Make this the most challenging
Of places for a walk.

Our energy is waning,
The pace begins to slow;
Can it be that we still have
The return trip to go?!

Note. If time allows, you can reverse the order of the environments, asking the children to continue with the return trip. You won't be able to do it in rhyme, but making the return trip provides an opportunity for repetition with some variety.

Getting Nowhere

Background Information.   Talk to the children about the difference between locomotor and nonlocomotor movement (locomotor is movement that transports the body from one place to another; nonlocomotor movement occurs while the body remains in place). Explain, however, that a number of locomotor movements (e.g., walking and running) can be performed *in place*. And that's what they're going to experiment with in this activity.

Activity.   Ask the children to perform the following locomotor skills *in place*. To add interest to the activity, include one of the variations, also listed, to each skill. Then every time you repeat this activity, you can mix and match the variations and skills differently.

Skills	*Variations*
Walking	In slow motion
Running	Very quickly
Jumping	As though on hot sand
Hopping	With a limp
Galloping	Frantically
Skipping	In a happy-go-lucky way

The Parade

Background Information.   Talk to the children about the parades they've seen. What was in them? Were there animals? What kind? What musical instruments did they see and hear? Discuss all of the possibilities mentioned here.

Activity.   Beforehand, you'll need to write the names of various people and things found in parades on scraps of paper. Place these in a container and let the children each draw one. They then form a ''parade,'' depicting whatever person or thing they've drawn. Possibilities include these:

Drummers (bass and snare)   Horses

Flutists   Fire engines

Trumpeters   Flag bearers

Trombonists   Banner carriers (must be an even number)

Cymbal players   Baton twirlers

Saxophonists   Floats

chapter 3 Seasons

- autumn
- winter
- spring
- summer

AUTUMN

Autumn Leaves

Background Information. The changing colors of the leaves and their inevitable fall from the trees are what we usually think of first when we consider autumn. Talk to the children in basic terms about what happens to the leaves—how the cool nights cause the leaves to change from green to bright orange, yellow, gold, or red, and how the autumn winds eventually blow them from their branches.

Activity. Tell the children that they're going to pretend to be autumn leaves. First, they're green, and they're hanging on branches. Then, the weather gets cooler and the leaves change colors. Suddenly, the wind begins to blow (you can pretend to be the wind if you like). The leaves are separated from their branches and begin to fall to the ground—but another gust of wind sends them twirling in the air. After a while, the wind stops and the leaves land on the ground. Finally, someone (you!) comes along and rakes all the leaves into a great big pile!

"Picking Apples"

Background Information. Autumn is apple-picking time in many parts of the country. Talk to the children about orchards (if they've never been to an orchard, they may think apples come from supermarkets!), the process of picking apples, and the feel, smell, and taste of this freshly picked fruit.

Activity. The children are now ready to act out the following poem. Read it as slowly as you need to, so they can portray the action realistically.

> Just out of reach
> So high in the tree
> Is a juicy red apple
> Waiting for me.
>
> Get on my toes
> And stretch up my hand,
> But I can't reach no matter
> How tall I stand.

So I must jump
As high as I can
'Til I have that apple in
My little hand!

I make it shine;
My job is complete.
My juicy red apple is
Ready to eat!

The School Year Begins

Background Information.   In North America, the month of September brings both the beginning of autumn and the start of the school year. Talk to the children about the first day of school. Discuss all the things parents and children do to prepare for the new school year, like buying pencils and paper, a lunch box, and new clothes. What else comes to the children's minds when they consider school?

Activity.   This is a being and doing activity, in which the children alternate between pretending to *be* something and pretending to *do* something. Ask them to show you the following:

Being	*Doing*
A pencil	Sharpening a pencil
A lunchbox	Packing a lunch
A sweater	Putting on a sweater
A blackboard	Writing on a blackboard
A ruler	Measuring something

Squirrels

Background Information.   Talk to the children about squirrels—how they look and how they move. What do squirrels eat? How do they look when they're eating? Then explain that, during autumn, many animals (including squirrels) begin collecting and storing food (mostly nuts) for the winter so they'll have enough to eat until spring.

Activity.   Ask the children to show you how a squirrel would do the following:

Swish its tail	Leap from one tree to another
Climb a tree	Hold nuts in its mouth
Eat food from between its paws	Bring food to a nest in a tree

The Nature of Autumn

Background Information.   When we think of nature and autumn, there are several things that come to mind: cooler temperatures, windy days, falling leaves, pumpkins, and the like. What do the children think of? What do they like best about autumn?

Activity.   Ask the children to show you how they would move if they were the following:

The wind
Falling leaves
Feeling chilly
Raking leaves

Trying to walk against the wind
Playing in the leaves
Picking and carrying a huge pumpkin

WINTER

LEARNING OBJECTIVES: To foster greater appreciation for all winter has to offer, both indoors and out; to encourage children to consider the nature of winter.

"Winter Sports"

Background Information. Winter in cold climates lends itself to a number of outdoor activities, three of the most popular being skiing, skating, and sledding. Talk to the children about the differences between these activities, especially emphasizing the movements each requires.

Activity. Teach the children the following song, performed to the tune of "Farmer in the Dell." Then ask them to act out the sport being sung about in each verse. (Leave enough time between verses to encourage them to adequately portray each sport.) The song is as follows:

> Sledding down the hill,
> Sledding down the hill,
> Hi-ho away I go,
> I'm sledding down the hill!
>
> **Second verse:** Skiing down the hill
>
> **Third verse:** Skating 'cross the ice

Alternate Activity. Play a recording of a waltz (Emil Waldteufel's *Skater's Waltz* and Johann Strauss's *Blue Danube* are perfect), and ask the children to imagine they're figure skating in the winter Olympics. Such skating would involve not only grace and elegance, but also well-executed jumps and turns.

Hibernation

Background Information. Because the normal food supply of certain birds and animals is not always available during winter months, these creatures must hibernate. What they're actually doing is lowering their normal body temperatures in order to save energy, but children usually think of animals' hibernation as "going to sleep" for the winter.

Talk to the children about hibernation and some of the animals that practice it. Bears, for instance, often hibernate in caves, while groundhogs hibernate under the ground, burrowing through tunnels to reach their nests.

Activity. Ask some of the children to form "tunnels" that lead underground. The remaining children act as groundhogs, making their way from the surface of the ground, through the tunnels, and to their nests. When the groundhogs reach their nests, they curl up and go to sleep. (If time permits, you can repeat this activity, having the children reverse roles.)

Alternate Activity.   Divide the children into groups of three. Two of the children form a cave, while the third pretends to be a bear. With the onset of winter, the bear makes its way into the cave and falls asleep. (If possible, let every child have a chance to be a bear.)

Baby, It's Cold Outside!

Background Information.   Asking children to experience (or imagine) opposites, in alternation, is a wonderful way to make a point! In this exercise, the children are going to consider the cold by comparing it with its opposite.

Talk to the children about cold and hot. What things are the coldest? The hottest? How do cold and hot make them feel? How do their bodies react to each?

Activity.   Tell the children they're going to really have to use their imaginations for this activity. Then ask them to show you how their bodies would move or look if they were the following:

Outside in the freezing cold
Soaking in a hot tub
Outdoors in the winter without mittens
Warming their hands by a fireplace
Drinking ice water on a winter day
Drinking hot cocoa
Rubbing their faces with snow
Pressing a wet, hot washcloth to their cheeks
Making angels in the snow without a jacket
Snuggling in a nice, warm bed

Think Snow!

Background Information.   Children love snow and all that it has to offer. Ask your children what things they like best about snow. Have they ever built a snowman? How did they do it? What did it look like when it was all done? What happens to a snowman when the days are sunny and the weather gets a little warmer? Talk to them about snow-flakes and how no two are alike, and discuss what happens to a snowball when it's rolled downhill, gathering more snow.

Activity.   With this exercise, the children are going to pretend to be snow in a variety of forms. Ask them to show you how they would look if they were the following:

A snowflake falling
A snowball that starts small and gets bigger as it rolls down a hill
A snowman being built (from beginning to end)
A snowman melting

"The Fireplace"

Background Information.   Keeping warm is a major part of winter, and many people keep their homes warm with fireplaces. Ask the children how many of them have fireplaces or wood stoves at home. Talk to them about the work involved in chopping and stacking wood and in building a fire. What does fire look like? How does it move?

Activity.   The children act out the following song, which is sung to the tune of "London Bridge."

> This is how I chop the wood,
> Chop the wood, chop the wood.
> This is how I chop the wood
> On this wintry day.
>
> **Second verse**: Stack the wood
>
> **Third verse**: Carry the wood
>
> **Fourth verse**: Build a fire

Note. The fourth verse can include crumpling newspaper, laying the wood, and striking the match.

Alternate Activity.   With the children acting as pieces of wood, arrange them in an imaginary fireplace. The "kindling" can be lying on the floor, with the rest of the "wood" arranged at various levels around the kindling (kneeling, squatting, standing bent, and standing straight). You then pretend to light a match at the kindling level, and the children, one level at a time, begin to move like flames "dancing."

Note. Although pieces of wood are usually piled on top of each other, you'll want to arrange the children so they're near each other but not quite touching. Or you can emphasize the importance of the "pieces of wood" leaning gently against one another.

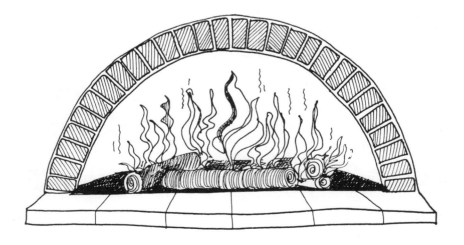

SPRING

LEARNING OBJECTIVES: To foster appreciation for all spring has to offer; to develop a better understanding of the transition from winter to summer.

"Seeds"

Background Information. Explain to the children that seeds lie dormant in the ground throughout the winter. In spring, with the return of warm temperatures and the help of both the rain and the sun (''April showers bring May flowers''), seeds slowly begin to grow into flowers, first poking up through the ground and then gradually blossoming into their full glory.

Activity. Teach the children the following song, sung to the tune of ''The Itsy Bitsy Spider.'' Then, once you've sung it together, ask them to get on the floor and to make themselves into the smallest shapes possible, imagining they're tiny seeds in the ground. Move throughout the room, pretending to be the rain falling on each of the seeds. Next, acting as the sun, ''shine'' on the seeds, warming them up. The seeds eventually begin to grow—very slowly—eventually poking through the ground and blossoming into the most beautiful flowers on earth! The song is as follows:

> The itsy bitsy seed
> Lies deep within the ground.
> First comes the rain;
> Feel it falling down.
> Then out comes the sun
> And dries up all the rain,
> And the itsy bitsy seed
> Can start to grow again.

Melting Snowmen

Background Information. Ask the children how many of them built snowmen during the past winter. What did they look like? Were they big or small? What shape are most snowmen? What happens to the snowmen when spring comes and the weather gets warmer?

Activity. Ask the children to each pretend to be a snowman—just like one they might have built. Can they make themselves as round as possible? Once they've assumed the shapes they want, you become the shining sun. Ask the children to imagine that their

snow is getting warmer and warmer, until it finally begins to melt. The snowmen continue melting—very slowly!—until they're nothing but puddles on the ground.

Note. This activity can be performed immediately after Seeds as a study in contrast. Or it can be used as a relaxation exercise.

Butterflies

Background Information.   *Metamorphosis* is the word used to describe the life cycle of a butterfly. There are four stages: egg, caterpillar, chrysalis, and butterfly. The egg is very tiny and is usually laid under the leaf of a plant. The caterpillar is long and tubular in shape, and it has six eyes on each side and several pairs of legs. The chrysalis hangs from a tree by a silken thread and represents the "resting" stage; the butterfly begins to form inside the chrysalis. And, finally, there is the adult butterfly, with its bright, colorful wings, exactly the same on both sides. While resting, the butterfly holds its wings vertically, almost touching each other over the back of the body.

Activity.   Tell the children they're going to act out the life cycle of a butterfly, beginning with the egg. Ask them to make themselves as small as they can, becoming a tiny egg under a leaf. (You might choose to have half the children act as eggs, while the others kneel over them, representing leaves.) The "eggs" then turn into long and tubular caterpillars. Ask them to show you how caterpillars move. Can several of the children join together to form one long caterpillar? Next, the children experience the motionlessness of being a chrysalis, either by lying on the floor or by pretending to hang from the branch of a tree from a silken thread. (Some children could portray trees and others the thread.) Finally, the children move like butterflies—either in flight, drinking nectar from flowers, or resting at night, with wings in a vertical position.

Free at Last!

Background Information.   Talk with the children about how it feels to be all bundled up in winter clothes. What kinds of clothes must they wear in winter? Possibilities include sweaters, heavy jackets, snowsuits, scarves, mittens, hats, heavy socks, boots, and earmuffs. Now ask them how spring makes them feel. Do they enjoy shedding all those extra clothes?

Activity.   Ask the children to pretend they're dressed in all of the items you've discussed. Are they warm? Do they feel like they weigh a lot more than usual? Now ask them to show you what it would look like to remove those items, one by one. Do they feel cooler? More free?

Once the children are "unencumbered," ask them to show you how that freedom makes them feel like moving. Does it make them feel like dancing or skipping? (For older students, this can be a good opportunity to introduce or practice this locomotor skill.)

Note. This activity could be accompanied by a piece of music with a light and airy feel. One suggestion: pieces from Bach's _Anna Magdalena Notebook._

"Spring Cleaning"

Background Information.   Spring is a time for renewal. Flowers and leaves return, as do the birds that have flown south for the winter. Windows are opened to the fresh spring air after months of being closed. And the warmth and the sunshine make people feel renewed, too—more energetic. So moms and dads often like to use that extra energy to renew their surroundings as well, to make their homes fresh and like new. That's called spring cleaning!

What household chores might family members have to do when spring cleaning? Possible responses include washing windows or floors, painting walls, shaking out carpets, putting up new curtains, vacuuming, and putting away winter clothes.

Activity.   Sing the following verses to the tune of "Whistle While You Work," as the children act out the movements involved. (The song should be sung _slowly!_)

>Smiling while you work
>To make the windows shine;
>Around and 'round
>And 'round and 'round
>To make them look so fine!
>
>Smiling while you work,
>You're vacuuming the rug.
>Go back and forth
>And back and forth—
>Yes, you deserve a hug!

Smiling while you work
To give the walls fresh paint.
Go up and down
And up and down
To make the house look quaint!

Smiling while you work,
New curtains look so nice.
We stretch and bend
And stretch and bend
To make home paradise!

SUMMER

LEARNING OBJECTIVES: To foster greater appreciation for all summer has to offer; to encourage children to consider the nature of summer.

Water Sports

Background Information. Summer is the time for water sports! Talk to the children about the sports listed here, asking if they've ever performed or watched any of them. What are the movements involved in each sport?

Activity. Giving them ample time to explore each, ask the children to show you the movements involved in performing the following sports:

Swimming
Waterskiing
Rowing a boat

Paddling a canoe
Surfing
Fishing

The Nature of Summer

Background Information. When we think of nature and summer, many images come to mind. Ask the children what they think of when they consider summer and nature. Be sure to specifically include a discussion of the images listed here.

Activity. Ask the children to show you, with their bodies, what they think the following look like:

The shining sun
A flower
A bumblebee
A tomato hanging on a vine
Gentle rain

Cornstalks rustling in the breeze
The heat
A fluffy white cloud
Grass

The Thunderstorm

Background Information. Thunderstorms are for some children a scary aspect of nature during the summer. But by talking about them with the children—and having them explore thunderstorms through movement—you can help alleviate any fears while broadening children's knowledge.

Explain, simply, that thunder and lightning result when hot air and cold air meet in the sky. Ask the children to describe thunder, lightning, storm clouds, heavy rain, and wind to you. What are the colors of storm clouds and lightning? What are their shapes? What are the sounds of rain, wind, and thunder?

Activity.   Ask the children to move as they imagine the following elements of a storm do.

Dark clouds
Heavy rain
Wind
Lightning
Thunder

Alternate Activity.   Ask the children to imagine they're dark clouds. The "clouds" begin to come together, a few at a time, in the center of the room (like storm clouds gathering). Then, when all of the clouds are together, a thunderstorm develops. Ask the children to move, as a group, like a thunderstorm.

The Picnic

Background Information.   Picnics are a popular activity during the summer. Ask the children if they've ever been on a picnic. Can they describe their picnics to you? Where were they held? What did they bring to eat? Did they have a picnic basket and a blanket? What do they like best about picnics?

Activity.   Children love stories, and they love to imagine themselves in them. So you're going to tell the following brief story, asking the children to act it out as you read. The story is this:

One warm, sunny day, the children of the [*Name of school or center*] decided to go on a picnic. So they made some sandwiches and packed them in picnic baskets. Then they set off for the park.

It felt so good to be outdoors! The sun was shining, and the air smelled so fresh.

When the children arrived at the park, they chose the perfect spot—on the grass, beneath the low-hanging branches of a willow tree—to spread their blanket. Then they all sat down on the blanket, opened up their picnic baskets, and ate the food they had packed.

When they were finished, the children picked up their napkins and scraps of food and threw them in the trash barrel. But then they were tired. So they went back to the blanket, and they lay down and fell asleep under the willow tree!

The Barbecue

Background Information. Barbecuing is the way many people cook a lot of their meals during the summer. Talk to the children about barbecuing—about the shapes and sizes of barbecue grills, the way charcoal looks (before and after it's lit), and the process involved in barbecuing. Be sure to specifically discuss the images listed here.

Activity. With this exercise, the children are going to pretend to be a number of things related to barbecues. Ask them to show you the following:

> The shape of a barbecue grill
> Lighter fluid being squirted from a container
> A match being struck and lit
> Coals heating up
> Something sizzling on the grill

chapter 4

HOLiDAYS

- Halloween
- Thanksgiving
- Hanukkah
- Christmas
- New Year's Day
- Valentine's Day
- Independence Day

HALLOWEEN

LEARNING OBJECTIVES: To stimulate the imagination; to help children deal with the scarier aspects of Halloween in a nonthreatening environment.

Halloween Shapes

Background Information.   Halloween, with its many images, provides a great opportunity to explore the element of shape. Ask the children what they think of when they hear the word *Halloween*, and then use their responses, as well as the images listed, as part of your activity.

Activity.   Ask the children to show you, with their bodies, the shapes of Halloween. Possibilities include these:

A witch's hat	A bat (the flying kind)
A pumpkin	A cat
A broom	A skeleton
A trick-or-treat bag	A ghost
A candle and flame	A candy bar
A cupcake	

If I Could Be . . .

Background Information.   Children love to pretend, and they almost always have a favorite person, character, or thing they like to pretend to be (though it can change from day to day!). Tell the children they're going to pretend it's Halloween night and that they can be absolutely anything they want. Then give them a few moments to decide what they'd most like to be.

Activity.   Ask the children, one at a time, what person or thing they most want to be on Halloween. Then, after a child has told you, ask her or him to show you how that person or thing moves. If time permits, you can also ask the rest of the class (as a whole) to show you *their* interpretations of each child's fantasy.

The Witch

Background Information.   Talk to the children about witches. Have they ever seen one in a book or movie or on television (perhaps in *Snow White* or *The Wizard of Oz*)? What do witches look like? What do they wear? How do they sound? Discuss the fact that, in stories, bad witches ride brooms and mix up "potions" in cauldrons. And be sure to mention such physical characteristics as gnarled hands and hunched backs.

Activity. The children are going to act out the creation of a potion, or witch's brew, from the conception of the idea to the finished product. Ask the children to show you a witch doing the following:

Wringing her hands as she plans her potion
Measuring ingredients into the cauldron
Stirring the brew
Tasting the brew (it's going to be hot!)
Adding more ingredients
Stirring and tasting again
Measuring the brew into a vial (or small container)
Flying off on her broom

Halloween Means . . .

Background Information. Halloween means different things to different children. Some are excited by the prospect of a school party. Others look forward to dressing up and pretending to be something or someone else. Some think only of the candy they're going to get. Still others are frightened by the idea of goblins and skeletons and such.

Talk to the children about what Halloween means to them. What do they like most about Halloween? Least? Why?

Activity. Ask the children to show you the following:

Being excited
Feeling scared
Walking as though scared
Putting on their costumes
Admiring their costumes in the mirror
Eating something yummy
Eating something yucky
Having a tummy ache after eating too much candy
Sharing their candy with friends

"Black and Orange"

Background Information. Black and orange are the traditional colors of Halloween. Discuss this with the children, and ask them what comes to mind when each of these colors is mentioned. Black is the darkest color there is, and orange is a very bright color. How do each of these colors make them feel?

Activity.   Ask the children to show you how the color black makes them feel like *moving*. How does the color orange make them feel like moving? How does *Halloween* make them feel like moving? Then ask them to move in those ways to the accompaniment of the following poem.

Black is oh-so-very dark—
The opposite of light.
Black cats, black hats, black sky above,
The color of the night!

Orange is so very bright—
Just like the shining sun.
Orange fruit and orange drinks,
A color meant for fun!

But put them both together,
And black and orange mean
The spookiest of holidays
The fun of Halloween!

THANKSGIVING

LEARNING OBJECTIVES: To develop an understanding of the background and meaning of this holiday and an appreciation for the "thanks" in Thanksgiving.

The Meal: Before and After

Background Information. The Thanksgiving Day dinner is a tradition as old as the holiday itself. And even though sharing the feast with family and friends is something to be eagerly anticipated, it requires a great deal of work (as do most worthwhile projects), both before and after. Discuss this with the children, asking them to tell you some of the chores that must be done.

Activity. Ask the children to show you how they would perform these jobs:

Rolling pie dough	Mashing potatoes
Peeling and slicing apples	Setting the table
Stuffing the turkey	Serving the meal
Basting the turkey	Clearing the table
Peeling potatoes	Washing dishes

Counting Blessings

Background Information. Explain to the children that the purpose behind Thanksgiving is to take some time to consider our blessings—to feel appreciation for all that we have. These blessings might include family, friends, beloved pets, good health, good food to eat, a home, and so forth.

Activity. Ask each child, in turn, what he or she is most grateful for (what his or her favorite thing in life is). Then ask her or him to *show* you that blessing through movement. If time permits, you can also ask the rest of the class (as a whole) to show you their interpretations of each child's blessing.

Pilgrims and Indians

Background Information. Talk to the children about the historical origins of Thanksgiving—how the pilgrims came to America, only to find the first winter very difficult. But the Indians taught them many things about finding and growing food, and that enabled the pilgrims to survive. The first Thanksgiving was a meal shared by the Indians and the pilgrims.

Activity. Divide the children into two equal groups of "pilgrims" and "Indians." Ask the pilgrims to stand side by side facing the Indians, who are also standing side by side. (There should be a pilgrim opposite every Indian, a few feet apart.) Each Indian is to act out the following, as though instructing the pilgrims. The pilgrim opposite then imitates the Indian's movements.

Possible actions can include the following:

Fishing   Picking corn
Shooting a bow and arrow   Shucking corn
Planting corn   Chopping wood

When all of that has been done, the pilgrims and Indians come forward to shake each other's hands.

Note. If time permits, you can ask the children to change roles, so everyone has a chance to "lead" and a chance to imitate. Or, the next time you perform this activity, you can be sure that the children play the opposite role.

The Food: Before and After

Background Information. Unless a child has had experience with the preparation of food, she or he is likely to think that certain foods arrive at the dinner table in their natural form. Talk to the children about all the foods mentioned below, discussing where they come from and the differences between their natural and cooked states.

Activity. Ask the children to show you, with their bodies, the way the following foods look in both their "before" and "after" states. Possibilities include these:

A cranberry and cranberry sauce   An apple and applesauce
A potato and mashed potatoes   A pumpkin and a pumpkin pie
A carrot and a cooked carrot slice A squash and cooked squash

Thanksgiving Things

Background Information. In this activity the children are going to pretend to be a number of inanimate objects associated with Thanksgiving. But what makes the activity especially challenging is that these inanimate objects are having something *done* to them. Talk in detail about the following, and feel free to add any others you or the children might think of.

Activity. Ask the children to show you how it would look if they were the following:

An ear of corn being shucked   An apple being sliced
Potatoes being mashed   A salad being tossed
Pie crust being rolled   A candle melting
A dish being washed

HANUKKAH

LEARNING OBJECTIVES: For Jewish children, these activities provide opportunities to experience and appreciate Hanukkah in a new way. For non-Jewish children, the activities offer familiarity with the holiday and an appreciation for traditions other than their own.

The Menorah

Background Information. Hanukkah is an eight-day celebration also known as the Festival of Lights. The menorah, a candle holder with nine candles, is a symbol of the holidays. The shāmmāsh is the center candle, and it's used to light each of the other eight candles—one for each night of the celebration. Explain all this to the children and, if possible, show a menorah or a picture of one.

Activity. Ask the children to hold their thumbs together, side by side, and to make fists with their remaining fingers. Their thumbs symbolize the shāmmāsh and their fingers the eight other candles. As you begin to count one to eight (slowly at first), the children lift their fingers, one at a time, symbolizing the lighting of the candles. They can then "extinguish" each candle by folding the eight fingers back toward their palms as you count backward from eight.

Note. Repeat this activity several times, varying the tempo of your counting.

"Eight Candles for Eight Nights"

Background Information. This is a counting activity that will help the children to remember the eight candles for the eight nights of Hanukkah.

Activity. Sing the following song to the tune of "Ten Little Indians," going slowly to allow the children to pretend to light (counting aloud as they do) the right number of candles. For example, if you've just sung "five," they pretend to light five candles as they count one to five.
The song is as follows:

> One, two, three little candles,
> Four, five, six little candles,
> Seven and eight little candles,
> One for every night!

The Candle

Background Information.   As the children are by now aware, the candle is an important symbol of Hanukkah. Talk to the children about candles—their shapes, what they're made of, how their flames move, and how they melt.

Activity.   Ask the children to each assume the shape of a candle. You then move around the room, "lighting" each candle individually. (How can the children show they've just been lit?) The children then pretend to burn for a while, before they begin melting. They should continue melting until the wax is just a puddle.

Note. You could use this as a relaxation exercise at the end of your movement class or at the end of the day.

A Festival of Lights

Background Information.   Because Hanukkah is the Festival of Lights, talk to the children about the shining of lights (including candles and stars, which are associated with this holiday). How does the light make them feel, as opposed to the dark?

Activity.   Ask the children to close and open their eyes a few times (varying the length of time they keep their eyes closed) as one way of experiencing dark versus light. Then explain that, for this activity, *closed* means dark and *open* means light, and ask how else they can show light and dark with their bodies. Possibilities include opening and closing the following:

Mouth	Knees
Hands	Feet
Arms	The body as a whole
Legs	

Star of David

Background Information.   Show the children a picture of the Star of David, explaining that this, too, is a Jewish symbol. (Or you could draw one for them: two triangles intersecting to create a six-pointed star.) Then talk to the children about the shape of the star.

Activity.   Ask the children to each show you, with their bodies, the shape of the Star of David. Can they show you how it would look if the star were shining brightly? Then ask them to pair off and to create the shape with a partner.

CHRISTMAS

LEARNING OBJECTIVES: To strengthen appreciation for the spirit of giving; to help the children more fully experience the joy that is part of this holiday.

Christmas Shapes

Background Information. Children can never have too much experience with the movement elements of shape and space—and Christmas, with its many images, certainly lends itself to the exploration of these elements. Talk to the children about the shapes of the images here—and feel free to add to the list!

Activity. Ask the children to show you, with their bodies, the shape of the following:

A Christmas tree

An ornament

A snowman

A bell

A chimney

A star

A reindeer

A Christmas present

The bow on top of the present

Tinsel

A wreath

A sled

"Stringing Popcorn"

Background Information. In these modern times, many children may never have strung popcorn for a Christmas tree. In fact, they may never have even seen such a thing. Describe this special decoration to them, beginning with the popping of the corn and ending with hanging the string on the tree. Explain that the string of popcorn is wrapped around the tree in "tiers," just as garland or a string of lights is.

Activity. Tell the children that you're going to make a string of popcorn—with *them* as the popcorn! Ask them to get into the smallest shape possible, each pretending to be a kernel of corn. You then move around the room, "turning on the heat" under all of the kernels, which begin to "pop."

When your popcorn is fully cooked, you link the pieces together, one at a time, by pretending to run a needle and thread from the fingertips of one child's hand to the next. (The children join hands, in other words.) Finally, when the string is complete, the children circle an imaginary tree (or a real one, if that's possible), singing the following song to the tune of "Here We Go 'Round the Mulberry Bush."

> Here we go 'round the Christmas tree,
> The Christmas tree, the Christmas tree.
> Here we go 'round the Christmas tree
> So early Christmas morning.

Alternate Activity. Once the ''popcorn'' has been strung, ask the children to find how many shapes the string can assume. They should try this as a circle (with all of their hands linked) and as a line (with two of the children letting go).

Being Santa

Background Information. Santa Claus is one of the things children love most about Christmas, and in this activity they're going to have a chance to ''be'' him. Talk to the children about Santa, asking them to describe him for you. What does he look like? What does he wear? What do they like best about him?

Activity. Reminding the children that their portrayals should be as realistic as possible, ask them to show you how Santa might do the following:

Walk

Drive his sleigh

Walk along a rooftop

Come down a chimney

Carry his bundle of presents

Arrange his presents around a tree

Hand out presents to children

Laugh!

A Christmas Dance

Background Information. This activity is based on the game of Statues, which requires the children to move while there is music playing and to freeze into ''statues'' when the music stops. It's a wonderful activity, in that it offers the children an opportunity to express themselves through ''improvisation.'' But because they think of it as a game rather than as dance improvisation, self-consciousness is alleviated. Thus the children might feel more comfortable with the idea of playing Statues (using Christmas characters) than with doing a Christmas dance.

Talk about the characters children will be asked to portray, discussing how each might move.

Activity. Put on a recording of Christmas music (preferably some that is both lively and familiar to the children), stopping and starting it at random intervals (lift the needle if it's a record, or press the pause button for a tape). Each time you stop the music, ask the children to become—and move like—a new Christmas character. Characters can include the following:

Santa Claus

A reindeer (Rudolph perhaps)

An angel

One of Santa's elves

Frosty the Snowman

The Spirit of Giving

Background Information.   Christmas is a time for giving—something children who anxiously look forward to *receiving* can easily overlook. You can help to emphasize the giving aspect by talking about it with the children. Do they have any plans for gift giving this Christmas? What are they giving, and to whom? If they could give one person absolutely anything in the whole wide world, what would they give and to whom? Why?

Activity.   Have the children stand in a circle, and explain that you're going to ask them to move in certain ways. But instead of doing movements all together, the children will do them in turns. In other words, one child performs a movement, "giving" it to the child beside him or her, and each child, all the way around the circle, repeats it. (You can offer the suggestions here—all with Christmas in mind—but each leading child has the opportunity to perform that movement in any way he or she chooses.)
   Possible suggestions include the following:

A handshake
Christmas lights blinking
A reindeer shaking its head
A bell ringing

Chopping down a Christmas tree
Waking up Christmas morning
A smile!

<u>Note</u>. Begin each round of movement with a different child.

NEW YEAR'S DAY

LEARNING OBJECTIVES: To develop an understanding
and appreciation for this "adult" holiday.

Happy New Year!

Background Information.   Discuss the meaning of this holiday with the children,
explaining that the New Year gives people a whole new year to look forward to! It's
fun and exciting to think of all the things you want to do in the coming year, so people
celebrate the arrival of this holiday in a lot of different ways.

   Some of the images that come to mind when we think of New Year's Eve and New
Year's Day are listed here. Talk about them with the children (their meanings as well
as their physical characteristics).

Activity.   Ask the children to pretend to be the following:

> A noisemaker (the unraveling kind)
> Confetti that has been tossed
> The ball in Times Square
> A clock
> A party hat on someone's head
> A calendar with its pages being turned

The Clock

Background Information.   Explain to the children that on New Year's Eve most adults
stay up late, looking forward to the stroke of midnight. That's the signal that the New
Year has officially begun. So a clock is an important part of the New Year celebration.

Activity.   You're going to be the clock in this exercise. You raise your right arm overhead
to the 12:00 position, with your left arm down, center front. You then bring your right
arm sideways and down in a smooth arc to center front, where it meets your left arm.
When your palms touch, that's 6:00. *Both* arms then separate and sweep out and up.
When they meet overhead at 12:00, the activity is over.

   The children, meanwhile, begin moving (in any way they want) when the clock begins
moving, and they stop when the clock strikes 12. They should match their tempo to the
speed of the clock's movements. Also, when the clock strikes six, they'll know the activity
is half over.

<u>Note</u>. Each time you perform this activity, you should vary the speed of the clock's hands.

Number One Day

Background Information. Explain to the children that there are 365 days in a year, and that January 1st is the first day of the first month. That's why it's called New Year's Day.

This activity will give the children a chance to explore the element of shape, while also giving some thought to numbers.

Activity. Ask the children to show you the number 1 with their bodies. How many *parts* of their bodies can they also make the number 1 with? (Possibilities include a finger, an arm, a leg, a foot, and a toe.)

There are 12 months in a year. Ask them to make a number 1 with their bodies, followed by a number 2.

There are 365 days in a year. Ask the children to make a number 3, a 6, and a 5.

After New Year's Day, there are 30 days left in January. Can they make a number 3, followed by a zero?

The Countdown

Background Information. Again, explain the importance of midnight on New Year's Eve, and help the children understand the anticipation leading up to midnight. Talk to them about the countdown that takes place during the 10 seconds before 12:00. (Have they ever heard a countdown, perhaps just before a space shuttle was launched?) And tell them that at the end of the countdown, at the stroke of midnight, people shout "Happy New Year!," cheer, and make a lot of noise.

Activity. Ask the children to freeze into a statue, get into a small shape on the floor, or stand with their hands over their eyes as you count backward from 10. Then, at "zero," they get to shout "Happy New Year," jump up and down, and make noise—until you begin the countdown again (when they resume their original positions). Repeat often, each time counting down at a different tempo.

Note. If you really want to give the children a chance to get some noise out of their systems, provide party noisemakers, musical instruments, or pots and pans and wooden spoons!

Resolutions

Background Information.   It can't be easy for a young child to understand all the talk about New Year's resolutions. But perhaps you can help by explaining that January 1st marks the beginning of a new year. Therefore, people like to "begin again" by making promises to do or improve some things in the coming year. For example, a person might make a promise (a resolution) to do something she or he hasn't gotten around to in the past year, like cleaning out the garage or painting the house.

Activity.   Ask each child, in turn, what he or she might resolve to do in the New Year and to then act it out for you. If time permits, you can also ask the rest of the class (as a whole) to show you their interpretations of each child's resolution.

VALENTINE'S DAY

LEARNING OBJECTIVES: To foster understanding of the reason for this holiday; to encourage the expression of feelings.

Feelings

Background Information. Explain to the children that the reason for Valentine's Day is so people can demonstrate that they care for one another. But it's okay (actually, it's great!) to show caring feelings all the time. In fact, it's a good idea to express all emotions—to communicate all of our feelings. What are some of the feelings the children experience sometimes? What makes them feel that way? How do they show those feelings?

Activity. Ask the children to show you how the following emotions make their bodies look or move. Feelings to include are these:

Happiness   Fear
Surprise   Pride
Sadness   Confusion
Anger   Love!

Playing Cupid

Background Information. Cupid is a fictional character who supposedly helps people fall in love by shooting them with his magical bow and arrows. He's red, looks like an angel (or cherub), has wings, and flies. (This can't be easy for the children to imagine, so it'd be helpful if you could show them a picture.) Discuss Cupid's characteristics and role as thoroughly as possible.

Activity. Ask the children to imagine that each of them is Cupid. Can they show you how Cupid would do the following?

Fly
Deliver Valentines
Shoot his magical arrows
Deliver flowers to people
Make people fall in love

Note. The last suggestion is wide open for individual interpretation. It will be interesting to see what each child comes up with!

Sending Cards

Background Information.   One of the most popular ways for people to show their affection on Valentine's Day is by sending cards. Who would the children like to send cards to next Valentine's Day?

Activity.   Explain to the children that they're going to act out the process of sending Valentine's Day cards, from choosing them to mailing them. Then ask them to pretend to do the following:

Buy a card at a store
Sign the card
Put it in an envelope
Seal the envelope

Address the envelope
Stamp the envelope
Mail the card

Alternate Activity.   Ask the children to pretend that *they* are the cards. What shape card do they want to be? Can they show you how they open and close? Can they pretend to slip into and out of an envelope? Can they pretend to go through the slot in the mailbox and then slide down?

"I Can Show I Care"

Background Information.   Again, Valentine's Day is specifically meant for showing others that we love and care for them. Who do the children care for? How do they show it?

Activity.   With this poem, the children have a chance to depict a variety of ways to display caring feelings. Although the poem refers to "I" and "you," each child should act out the poem as an individual, relating to an imaginary partner.

> I can show I care by
> Reaching out my hand,
> By giving you a gentle touch
> To say I understand.
>
> I can show I care by
> Giving you a smile,
> To make you feel like smiling, too,
> For just a little while.
>
> I can show I care by
> Giving you a hug—
> Wrap my arms around you 'til
> You feel so very snug!
>
> I can show I care by
> Giving you a kiss;
> For showing someone that you care
> A kiss can never miss!

For My Valentine

Background Information.   Tradition requires that we give something to the one special person we've chosen to be our "Valentine." Some of the traditional gifts are listed here. Talk to the children about the characteristics of each of them. Especially explain the last item on the list; when you give someone your "heart," what does that actually mean?

Activity.   Ask the children to pretend to be the following. But explain that you don't want to see just the *shape* of these things; you want to see the items actually *doing* something that typifies them. You can leave the choice of action to the children or you can make the suggestions offered in parentheses. Valentine's Day gifts can include these things:

A rose (blooming)   A card (opening)
A balloon (floating)   A ring (shining)
A box of candy (opening)   Your heart (beating)

INDEPENDENCE DAY

LEARNING OBJECTIVES: To help the children understand
this holiday more fully; to foster appreciation of the reason
for the celebration.

July 4, 1776

Background Information.   Explain to the children that it was on July 4, 1776, that
America won its independence from England—and that we've been celebrating Independence Day on the Fourth of July ever since. Also mention that July is the seventh month
of the year.

Activity.   Ask the children to show you the number 7 (for the month of July) with their
bodies. Give them enough time to explore the possibilities and then ask them to move
slightly to their left (if standing, they can take a step to the left; if lying, they can roll).
Now ask them to show you a number 4, followed by another move to the left. Can they
make a number 1? How about a number 7 again? (Each number is followed by a move
to the left.) Can they find another way to make a number 7? Finally, ask them to move
left once again and to show you a number 6. Now congratulate them—they've just made
July 4, 1776!

Alternate Activity.   Divide the children into groups of four, assigning each child a
number (1, 7, 7, and 6). Then ask the children in each group to arrange themselves to
form *1776.*

Let's March

Background Information.   Whether it's police officers in a parade or 18th-century revolu-
tionaries playing fife and drum, marching comes to mind when we think of the Fourth
of July. Talk to the children about marching and what makes someone a good marcher
(a tall, straight body, good rhythm, and so on).

Activity.   Put on a piece of marching music (John Philip Sousa marches are the most
well-known), and ask the children to march in the following ways:

   In place, with knees high
   In place, turning to the right (in one direction); to the left (in the other
      direction)
   Forward, swinging their arms
   Pretending to play the musical instrument of their choice

The American Flag

Background Information.   Talk to the children about the American flag. Do they know what colors it's made of? Do they know what's on it? What do the 50 stars represent? Have the children ever seen a flag being raised up a flagpole? Discuss some of the reasons a flag might be lowered to half-mast, the fact that there is a proper way to fold a flag, and the respect our flag deserves.

Activity.   Tell the children they're going to pretend to be a lot of different things associated with the flag. Then ask them to show you the following:

>   The shape of a flag
>   A star
>   A stripe
>   A flagpole
>   A flag being raised up a flagpole
>   A flag at half-mast
>   A flag waving proudly in the breeze
>   A flag being lowered down a flagpole
>   A flag being folded

Alternate Activity.   Divide the children into "stars" and "stripes" and have them form either several small flags or one large one!

The Parade

Background Information.   Parades are a Fourth of July tradition, and children love them! Talk to your children about the parades they've seen. Who and what was in the last parade they saw? Were there any animals in it? What things did they like best?

Activity.   Tell the children they're going to pretend to be a lot of different things that might be seen in a Fourth of July parade. Use some of the ideas they discussed with you, the list here, or a combination of both.
  Possibilities include the following:

A circus clown	A baton twirler
A soldier	A flagbearer
A fire engine	A cannon
A horse	

Celebration!

Background Information.   Talk to the children about the different ways people celebrate the Fourth of July: by having barbecues, going on picnics, watching parades and fireworks, and so forth. How do the children like to celebrate this holiday?

Activity. Ask the children to pretend to be the following, all of which are related to the celebration of Independence Day:

A flag being carried in a parade

A baton being twirled

A cannonball being fired from a cannon

A hot dog barbecuing on the grill

Fireworks!

A blanket being spread for a picnic

<u>Note</u>. If you can accompany this activity with a recording of Tchaikovsky's *1812 Overture*, it's all the more fun!

Chapter 5
Nature

- the sky
- weather
- birds
- more natural wonders

THE SKY

LEARNING OBJECTIVES: To familiarize children with and enhance their appreciation for various elements of nature having to do with the sky.

Clouds

Background Information.   Ask the children for their impressions of clouds. How many different kinds of clouds have they seen? What do they think clouds are made of? Have they ever sat looking up at the sky, watching the clouds form the shapes of objects or animals? (If possible, bring the children outside to do just that before this activity.)

Activity.   Ask the children to move like the following:

> Big fluffy clouds
> Wispy clouds
> Dark storm clouds
> Clouds drifting and slowly changing shape

Then, time permitting, ask the children to cooperate as a group, each beginning as a single cloud but gradually drifting together and apart, forming larger and then smaller clouds. Sometimes two ''clouds'' will drift together to form a floating shape; sometimes larger groups of clouds will join and separate.

Constellations

Background Information.   A constellation is a configuration of stars. Many constellations, to the eye or through a telescope, look like familiar shapes. Perhaps the most well-known constellations are those commonly called the Big Dipper and the Little Dipper. Have the children ever seen these? If possible, provide pictures of these and other constellations.

Activity.   Tell the children to pretend to be stars shining in the night sky. Then call out a number, no smaller than three and no larger than six. The children divide themselves into groups of that number and form ''constellations.'' What shapes can they make with that number of stars? Repeat this several times with different numbers.

Note. If one or two groups are left with fewer ''stars'' than you've called out, that's okay. These smaller constellations can add variety to the patterns in the sky.

Over the Rainbow

Background Information. *Webster's Third New International Dictionary* defines a rainbow as "an arc of a circle exhibiting in concentric bands the several colors of the spectrum and formed opposite the sun by the refraction and reflection of the sun's rays in drops of rain." But, to most of us, a rainbow is something wonderful that sometimes appears in the sky following a rainstorm.

Have the children ever seen a rainbow, either in pictures or in the sky? What shape was it? What colors were in it?

Activity. Instruct the children to each make the shape of a rainbow. Then ask them to take partners and make a two-person rainbow. Can they make rainbows standing up as well as lying down? Finally, ask them to join together as a group to form the biggest, most beautiful rainbow ever!

The Solar System

Background Information. Talk to the children about our solar system, which includes nine planets that revolve around the sun. They are, in the order of their distance from the sun (from nearest to farthest), Mercury, Venus, Earth, Mars, Jupiter, Saturn, Uranus, Neptune, and Pluto. Our solar system also consists of moons (our planet has only one) and stars.

If you want, you can show the children pictures of the planets, discussing the characteristics of each. Also, you should discuss solar and lunar eclipses, which are described in the activity.

Activity. For this activity, you'll need as many scraps of paper as there are children in your group. On each piece of paper, write the name of a planet or *sun*, *moon*, or *star*. The children draw one scrap apiece from a container. They then form a "solar system."

The sun, of course, will be in the center, "radiating light." The planets should each revolve around the sun at an appropriate distance (Mercury, for instance, will be the closest and Pluto the farthest away). The stars should "twinkle," and the moon revolves around the earth (from west to east, if you can work that into the activity). When the moon blocks the sun, a solar eclipse occurs; when the moon is in the earth's shadow, that's a lunar eclipse. How do the children want to depict solar and lunar eclipses?

Note. All this could take some time to work out, and it may take many repetitions before it's performed smoothly.

Sunrise/Sunset

Background Information. This is a great winding-down activity. Use it any time you feel the children need to relax a bit.

Talk to your group about the rising and setting of the sun. Have they ever watched a sunrise or sunset? Explain that the sun rises in the east and sets in the west, and it takes from early morning to early evening (and sometimes longer) for the sun to move from east to west. (If your children are old enough to understand, you can explain that the sun doesn't actually move; the earth revolves around *it*.)

Activity.   Ask the children to each get into a very small shape on one side of the room (the eastern side, if possible). They then pretend to be the sun *slowly* rising over the horizon. Once fully risen, the sun moves *in very slow motion*—shining all the while—across the "sky" (to the other side of the room) and begins setting, until it's no longer in sight.

<u>Note</u>. If you like, you can accompany this activity with a piece of slow, soft music, helping to set the mood and tempo.

WEATHER

LEARNING OBJECTIVES: To familiarize the children with various aspects of the weather; to make frightening aspects seem less so; to enhance appreciation of other aspects.

Lightning and Thunder

Background Information. What do the children think about thunder and lightning? Do they find them scary? Do they like to listen and watch during a thunderstorm from within the safety of their homes? If the children are old enough to understand, you may want to explain that lightning is the flash of light caused by a discharge of electricity from one cloud to another or from a cloud to earth. Thunder is the sound that follows the lightning and is caused by the expansion of air due to the electrical discharge. Although they won't understand it technically (any more than I do!), knowing that the phenomena have a scientific explanation may help alleviate any fear they have.

Activity. Ask the children to take partners. The partners then decide who is to be the thunder and who the lightning.

At a signal from you, the partners separate and begin moving about the room. While moving, however, thunder must be watchful of his or her partner—because you never know when lightning will ''strike.'' But every time lightning *does* strike, thunder must follow. In other words, the partner acting as lightning can choose any moment to ''strike'' —to move like lightning. The partner acting as thunder must then respond, moving in a way he or she feels depicts thunder. After a while, the partners reverse roles.

Note. Remind the children that flashes of lightning and rumbles of thunder can vary in intensity. Similarly, the number of seconds that pass between a flash of lightning and a rumble of thunder can also vary.

The Wind

Background Information. Talk to the children about the wind and its varying forces. A gentle breeze barely stirs the leaves on the trees. A light steady wind can offer relief on a hot day. A heavier wind can cause the trees to sway. A gale wind, as occurs during a hurricane, can cause major damage, including uprooting trees.

Activity. Ask the children to move as though they were a very gentle breeze. Then the breeze becomes a light wind. And, *gradually*, the strength of the wind grows stronger, until it's of gale force. The process then slowly reverses, until the children are once again pretending to be a breeze.

Alternate Activity. Once the children have experienced the varying forces required by the first activity, ask them to stand in a line, side by side. The first child begins as a gentle breeze, and each child down the line depicts a wind of slightly greater force, so that the last child in line is portraying a gale wind. The process can then be reversed. If time allows, you can also have the first child begin as the gale wind, so the children have a chance to experience the element of force differently.

Note. Because this exercise is executed sequentially, much like a ''wave'' performed by fans at a sporting event, you may have to offer some assistance, depending upon the ages of your children. If they have difficulty moving sequentially on their own, you can start at the beginning of the line, walking slowly toward the end and cuing each child in turn.

"Dance of the Snowflakes"

Background Information. Most children are fascinated by snow—even if they've never seen it. Discuss the properties of snow with your group: how no two snowflakes are ever alike, how snowflakes swirl in the wind, how they melt at first when falling upon a warmer earth, and how they begin to accumulate. What are the children's thoughts on snow? What do they like best about it?

Activity. Read the following poem to the children while they sit and listen. Then read it again slowly, asking the children to act out the images in each verse.

> Snowflakes drifting from the sky,
> Dancing lightly in the air.
> Falling, falling without a sound;
> Each is unique and rare.
>
> Snowflakes swirling in the wind
> In a dance they can't control.
> Higher, lower, around and 'round,
> Shivering in the cold.
>
> Snowflakes landing on the earth,
> Melting quietly from sight.
> Falling, falling until the ground
> Is blanketed in white.

The Rain

Background Information. Rainfall, like the wind, has varying degrees of force. A mist of rain is barely visible and gives the impression only that the air is moist. A drizzle is somewhat more evident than a mist, and a sprinkle more visible still.

Talk to the children about rain, discussing everything from a mist to a torrential downpour.

Activity. Ask the children to depict the following:

A mist	Wind-driven rain
A drizzle	A downpour
A sprinkle	Rain moving across a lake
Big heavy raindrops that plop	

Alternate Activity. Just as you did for The Wind, you can have the children stand in line and sequentially depict rainfall, from a mist to a torrential downpour and the reverse. Obviously rainfall will require different movements than wind did.

The Weather Report

Background Information. Do the children ever listen to the weather report on television or radio? Has bad weather ever changed or interrupted their plans? The weather report— which is sometimes wrong and sometimes right—predicts many different occurrences, which can vary according to area. Discuss with your group all of the weather elements listed here. Some the children have already experienced; others will be new and may require explanation.

Activity. Ask the children to move like each of the following elements of the weather:

Steady rain
Sunshine
A hurricane
Freezing cold
Fog rolling in
Sleet
Hail
A tornado
Heat lightning
The 3 H's: hot, humid, and hazy

BIRDS

LEARNING OBJECTIVES: To foster respect and appreciation for our feathered friends.

It's a Bird's Life

Background Information. All of the children will have *seen* birds, but they may not have paid particular attention to their habits. Talk to your group about the activities listed here, describing them in as much detail as possible. Have the children ever witnessed birds doing any of these things?

Activity. Ask the children to pretend to be birds doing the following:

> Splashing in a bird bath
> Eating seed at a feeder
> Cracking a sunflower seed on a branch
> Building a nest
> Feeding a baby bird
> Flying south
> Sleeping in the nest

Woody Woodpecker

Background Information. If your children are familiar with the cartoon character of Woody Woodpecker, then they have an idea of what a woodpecker looks like. (Woody, with his famous red crest and familiar call, is based on the large, seldom-seen pileated woodpecker; but there are several other kinds of woodpeckers as well.) If your children don't know who Woody Woodpecker is, you should probably provide a photo of a woodpecker—preferably one that is clinging to a tree, ready to do what it's named for.

Explain to the children that woodpeckers use their very strong beaks to peck at the bark or wood of trees for two reasons: to drill for insects for food and to dig holes for their nests. Have they ever seen or heard a woodpecker pecking at a tree? It's very rhythmic and makes a fairly loud sound.

Activity. This exercise offers an opportunity for the children to practice with rhythms and with their listening skills. Pretending to be woodpeckers drilling at trees, they'll "peck" in echoing response to the rhythms you establish. For instance, you clap three times at a slow tempo, and each child uses his or her head to peck three times, at the same tempo, saying aloud, "Peck, peck, peck." Repeat each pattern at least once, at a bit faster tempo if the children can handle it.

<u>Note</u>. You'll want to choose rhythm groupings according to the age and experience of the children in your class. Generally speaking, the younger the group, the shorter and slower the rhythms should be.

The Hummingbird

Background Information.   The ruby-throated hummingbird is the smallest of all birds and is the only bird that can fly backward as well as hover, like an insect, in one spot. Hummingbirds are constantly in motion, perching only briefly to rest or when they're at the nest. Hummingbirds got their name because, while they're flying, their wings make humming sounds. They feed at large tubular flowers, among others, and are also attracted to feeders filled with sugar water.

Activity.   Ask the children to perform the following actions like a hummingbird would:

Flit from flower to flower

Fly backward

Drink from a feeder

Hover

Note. Because the hummingbird's wings are always in motion—and move very swiftly—you should include pauses on twigs or at the nest between the above activities, or when you sense your hummingbirds need a brief rest.

"Wise Old Owl"

Background Information.   Show the children a picture of an owl, and talk about this bird's characteristics. Point out the owl's short, crooked beak, its large, bright eyes, and the sharp talons it uses to grip the tree branches it perches on. Other traits you might point out: the owl's ability to swivel its head and the fact that it's mostly nocturnal. Also, be sure to mention that the owl has a reputation for being very wise and that its call sounds like a *who-o-o*.

Activity.   Have the children sit in a circle. Then choose one child to be the "wise owl." That child pretends to be perched on a tree limb and closes her or his eyes. Once the owl's eyes are closed, you point to a child who must leave the circle and hide in a pre-determined place. When that child is hidden, the owl opens its big eyes, looks around, and chants:

> Who, who, who is missing?
> Whoever could it be?
> [*Child's name*]—that's who's missing
> My wise old eyes can see!

Repeat the activity until every child has had a chance to be the owl.

Alternate Activity.   If your group is too small to make the first activity challenging—or if you'd simply like another option—ask the children to identify a missing *object*. Assemble several items in the middle of the circle, pointing to and naming each one (the younger the children, the fewer the items you should select). Then, once the appointed owl has closed its eyes, remove one item and place it behind your back. Of course, then the owl will be chanting *what* instead of *who*, but that's okay!

The Early Bird

Background Information. "The early bird catches the worm" is a common saying that actually has nothing to do with birds. But some birds do eat worms, while others feast on a variety of other delicacies, from thistle to fish to snakes.

Talk to the children about the following birds and their feeding habits:

- Pigeons can often be seen in the park, eating breadcrumbs tossed to them by their human friends.
- Kingfishers are pigeon-sized and hover or perch over water until a fish is visible. They then dive straight down for their prey.
- There are several different kinds of hawks, but many of them feed on mice, snakes, and frogs. Some sit quietly on a low perch, waiting for their prey and then dropping down swiftly. Others soar over open country and then swoop down once they've spotted prey.
- Baby birds of all kinds wait in their nests—sometimes not very patiently—for mother or father to bring them food (usually insects). They then open their beaks as wide as possible so the food can be dropped in.
- Many tree-clinging birds, like some woodpeckers, nuthatches, and creepers, move up and down the trunk of a tree, probing the bark for insects.
- Robins (properly called American robins) can often be seen foraging on the ground for worms.

Activity. Ask the children to portray each of these birds in search of food. Feel free to add any others that come to mind!

MORE NATURAL WONDERS

LEARNING OBJECTIVES: To promote awareness of and appreciation and respect for various aspects of nature.

Water, Water Everywhere

Background Information. Humans tend to have a fascination with water. We like to ride on it, play in it, and just sit and look at it. This activity deals with many forms of water that haven't already been covered in previous chapters. Talk to the children about the list here, discussing the characteristics of each form of water as well as the similarities and differences between them.

Activity. Ask the children to move as though they were the following:

A babbling brook	A water hose
A winding river	A geyser
River rapids	A choppy lake
A waterfall	A calm lake
A lawn sprinkler	

"To Bee or Not to Bee"

Background Information. *Pollination* is a concept a bit too advanced for young children to grasp. But they can understand that bees feed on the pollen and nectar in flowers and plants. And by moving from flower to flower and plant to plant, they spread the pollen with their bodies and help the plants and flowers grow. They also use the nectar they feed on to produce honey. So bees are extremely helpful insects. (Perhaps that knowledge will help alleviate any fear of bees the children may have.)

Activity. Teach the children the following, sung to the tune of "Row, Row, Row Your Boat." Then have them sing it as they pretend to be bees.

> Buzz, buzz, buzz around
> From plant to flower to tree;
> Spreading pollen everywhere,
> That is my job, you see.
>
> Buzz, buzz, buzz around,
> It's time to make honey.
> That's the very useful life
> Of a busy bee!

Alternate Activity. Rimsky-Korsakov's *Flight of the Bumblebee* is a wonderful piece of classical music that children truly enjoy. If you can get hold of a copy, play it for your children as they pretend to be bees.

Mountain, Mountain, Volcano

Background Information. A volcano is a hill or mountain composed partly or completely of molten or hot rock, which issues, along with steam, from a vent in the earth's crust. Lava is the fluid rock that is spewed when a volcano erupts. A volcano often has a depression or crater at its top. Vesuvius is probably the most famous volcano in history, and Mt. St. Helens is our best-known volcano in America.

Show the children pictures if possible, and ask for their impressions of what happens when a volcano erupts.

Activity. This activity is somewhat similar to ''Duck, Duck, Goose,'' in that you will be tapping the children's heads and saying either *mountain* or *volcano*. But that's where the similarity ends, as here there'll be no chasing or elimination.

Ask the children to scatter on the floor and to form the shapes of mountains. Also ask them to close their eyes and to keep them closed until they're designated to be a volcano. You then tiptoe quietly among the children, tapping each one on the head and saying either *mountain* or *volcano*. The mountains will remain as they are. The volcanos, however, will ''erupt.'' After erupting, each volcano turns into lava, which spews from the crater and flows to the ground.

Continue with the activity until everyone has had a chance to erupt.

Note. Vary the number of mountains you designate between volcanos so the children will never know when to expect to be the latter.

Fire

Background Information. Fire is a natural wonder that has certainly proven to be both helpful and harmful. Talk to the children about the many uses of fire (e.g., cooking, heating homes, campfires) and about its potential dangers (e.g., getting burned with matches, homes and buildings burning, forest fires). Also discuss fire's characteristics: its color(s), ''size,'' and movement.

Activity. Ask the children to move as though they were the following:

> A match being struck
> The flickering flame of a candle
> A campfire
> A flame being raised and lowered on a gas stove
> A bonfire
> A fire spreading
> A forest fire out of control
> A flame dying out

Reptiles and Amphibians

Background Information.   A reptile is an animal that crawls or moves on its belly (a snake, for example) or on small short legs (like a lizard). An amphibian lives both in and out of the water (like a frog).

Many adults aren't particularly crazy about reptiles and amphibians, but children tend to be attracted to them. Talk to your group about snakes, lizards, and frogs. What do they think about these creatures? If they don't know what a lizard looks like and you don't have a picture, describe lizards to them, perhaps using dinosaurs as a basis for comparison.

Activity.   Simply ask the children to pretend to be snakes, lizards, and frogs. After they've had a chance to experiment on their own, you can make various suggestions for movement. Possibilities include the following:

> Catching an insect with a flick of the tongue
> A snake wrapping itself around the limb of a tree
> A frog swimming
> A frog hopping from one lily pad in a pond to another
> A lizard hiding under a rock

Alternate Activity.   Leap-Frog is an age-old game that has never lost its appeal for children. Why not play a game with your group and give the children further cause to think about frogs?

chapter 6

animals

- pets
- forest animals
- farm animals
- jungle animals

PETS

LEARNING OBJECTIVES: To help children consider and more fully appreciate the role of pets in our lives; to foster greater respect for domestic animals.

It's a Dog's Life

Background Information. Your children should all be, to various extents, familiar with dogs. Discuss the various canine traits and the way dogs move when they perform the activities listed here.

Activity. Stressing realism, ask the children to show you how a dog moves when it does the following:

Wags its tail   Begs
Fetches a newspaper   Plays catch with a Frisbee
Shakes hands   Rolls over
Buries a bone

"Pretty Birdie"

Background Information. Talk to the children about the various kinds of birds that can be pets and about the pleasures involved in having a bird. Do any of the children have birds at home? Can they describe them for the class? What kinds of things do they do? Do they do any of the things listed here?

Activity. Teach the children the following song, sung to the melody of "Twinkle, Twinkle, Little Star":

> Pretty birdie on your swing,
> How I love to hear you sing.
> With your feathers oh-so-bright
> You can make my cares seem light.
> Pretty birdie on your swing,
> How I love to hear you sing!

After the children have sung the song a couple of times, ask them to show you how a bird performs the following:

Swinging on its swing   Flapping its wings
Eating birdseed   Flying
Looking at itself in the mirror   Singing!

Cats

Background Information.   Although there are a number of characteristics considered typical of felines, cats, like people, all have personalities distinctly their own. Do the children have cats at home? What kind of personalities do they have? How do they move when they behave in the ways listed here?

Activity.   Stressing realism, ask the children to show you how a cat moves when it is behaving in the following ways:

Playing with a toy	Being afraid of something
Loving	Curling up to go to sleep
Stalking prey	Being lazy
Cleaning itself	

Turtles

Background Information.   Turtles are special animals, in that they are among the slowest of creatures and they have the ability to pull their bodies inside their shells. If possible, provide a picture of a turtle; then talk to the children about turtles and their characteristics. Have the children ever seen or had a turtle? How did it move?

   Moving slowly is not an easy task for young children, as it requires a great deal of control. But because pretending comes naturally to them, exploring the movements of a turtle provides an excellent opportunity to practice slow-motion moving.

Activity.   Ask the children to first assume the shape of a turtle and to show you how a turtle hides inside its shell. Then ask them to come out of their "shells" and show you how slowly a turtle moves. (You can perhaps designate beginning and ending points for them. But emphasize they're to reach the "finish line" *slowly*.)

Note. If you have an especially competitive class, you might ask them to show you which turtle can move the slowest. But be sure to offer praise and congratulations to *all* the turtles!

"If I Could Have Any Pet I Want"

Background Information.   With this activity, you can stress the importance of choosing a pet carefully. Talk to the children about the pets mentioned in the poem (and others, if you'd like), discussing both the responsibilities and joys involved in having them. Do the children have any of these pets at home? Do they help take care of them? What are some of their most predominant characteristics? How do they move?

Activity.   Read the following poem slowly, giving the children ample time to pretend to be the animal discussed in each verse. Because there are several pets mentioned in the fifth verse, you'll have to read it even slower than the others. For the last verse, the children can simply listen, recite the lines with you, or move like their favorite pets. The poem is as follows:

If I could have any pet I want,
It'd be so hard to choose—
I'd like to have a puppy dog
But he might chew up my shoes!

I'd like to have a furry kitten
Who would snuggle up and purr,
But then I know that come the spring
She would start to shed her fur!

Maybe tropical fish would be nice—
I'd watch them swim all day.
But I might have to clean their tank
When I'd rather go and play!

A hamster, a gerbil, or a mouse
Might make a real good pet.
But if it happened to get sick
Could I take it to the vet?

Still, puppies are fun, and loving, too;
Tropical fish are pretty.
Hamsters, gerbils and mice are cute,
And I would love a kitty!

Yes, it might be work to have a pet,
But they sure are lots of fun.
They also make the best of friends—
So why not have more than one?!

FOREST ANIMALS

LEARNING OBJECTIVES: To familiarize the children with forest animals and their environment; to foster respect and compassion for these creatures.

Skunks, Raccoons, and Foxes

Background Information. Pictures of these three animals would be very helpful. But if you don't have pictures available, you can describe skunks, raccoons, and foxes to your children. (They've each probably seen at least one of them.) Focus especially on the skunk's odor, which it uses to deter potential enemies; the raccoon's mask, which makes the animal look like a bandit; and the fox's beautiful, long, fluffy tail.

Activity. Explain to the children that every time you say the word *skunks*, they should hold their noses. When you say *raccoons*, they should make a mask over their eyes with their hands. And when you say *foxes*, they should make a tail with one or both arms.

Begin chanting these three words very slowly at first, giving the children time to get used to the activity. Then gradually pick up the pace. The faster you go, the more confusing—and more fun—it'll become!

<u>Note</u>. If you have a very young group of children, saying the animal's names in the same order every time will create less confusion. But with an older group (*or* a young group that's repeated this activity often), you should mix it up, sometimes saying the names in the same order and sometimes not.

The Bear

Background Information. Did any of the children see the movie "The Bear?" Have any of them seen a bear in person, perhaps at a zoo? Explain that you're not talking about polar bears here, who live in arctic regions, but about the kinds of bears that live in forests.

Discuss all of the habits listed here, talking especially about the movement involved. For instance, a bear does not climb a tree as a person does. Instead, the bear generally uses its front legs and back legs, in alternation, to shimmy up a tree.

Activity. Ask the children to pretend to be bears performing the following activities:

Walking on four legs
Walking on hind legs
Climbing a tree
Crossing a fallen tree trunk

Catching a fish in a river
Shaking water from its coat
Sleeping in its cave

"The Deer and the Moose"

Background Information. Although they are members of the same family, there are differences between the deer and the moose, the most notable being size. Also, while all moose have antlers, not all deer do. Most male deer have antlers, but only a few types of females do.

Show the children pictures of a deer and a moose, and talk to them about the differences between the two.

Activity. As you read this playfully "argumentative" poem, the children alternate between pretending to be a moose and a deer. Every time they hear the word *moose*, they should make themselves as large as they can and use their hands to demonstrate antlers. When the word *deer* is spoken, they should be smaller and can use a hand or hands to show the deer's tail. On the final two lines, the children should don "horns" and "run away."

The poem is as follows:

> I just saw a deer behind that tree
> And don't you know she was looking at me!
>
> That was no deer—it's plain to see
> That was a moose, as big as can be!
>
> A deer, I say, with a tail of white
> And eyes that shine in the dark of night!
>
> It was a moose, I'm sure I'm right—
> The animal had tremendous height!
>
> A deer or a moose—what silly chatter;
> The deer is smaller; the moose is fatter.
> The moose has antlers like a ladder;
> The deer moves softly, pitter-patter!
>
> Well, you must agree we will never know
> Gigantic bull moose or spotted doe.
> It could have been a *buffalo*
> Whatever it was left long ago!

Note. If you can speak in two different voices, pretending to be the "debaters" quoted in the poem, you'll ensure even greater enjoyment for the children! Also, with subsequent repetitions of this activity, you should read the poem more and more quickly, making it increasingly challenging!

Bunny-Hop

Background Information. Technically, to hop on two feet is to *jump* (hopping is performed on one foot at a time). Yet, when we think in terms of bunnies and rabbits, we think of their method of locomotion as hopping. (Of course, they use *four* feet, so who knows what that should be called!) With this activity, you're going to ask the children to, among other things, hop like rabbits; and it'll be up to them whether they want to move on two feet or on "all fours."

Talk to the children about rabbits—their traits and the way they move. What do rabbits look like?

Activity.   Ask the children to show you the following:

> Rabbit ears
> A rabbit's tail
> A rabbit wiggling its nose
> A rabbit eating lettuce
> A rabbit washing its face

Now ask the children to show you how a rabbit moves (hops), occasionally having them stop and sniff the air (for food or the possibility of danger!). When the children have moved long enough, ask them to show you a rabbit ducking into its hole in the ground.

Dance of the Animals

Background Information.   So far, the children have pretended to be rabbits, bears, raccoons, skunks, foxes, deer, and moose. Review the characteristics of these animals and then talk about others that live in forests, providing pictures whenever possible. Other forest animals might include squirrels, chipmunks, snakes, mice, and moles.

Activity.   Ask the children to choose the forest animal they would most like to be. Then put on a recording of a lively, upbeat piece of music, asking the children to move like the animals they represent (or to dance like they think the animals would).

Alternate Activity. Another option is to play Statues, randomly stopping and starting the music and asking the children to move only while the music is playing. When the music stops, they must freeze into statues of their animals. If you choose this activity, you might also choose to assign one animal to the entire group for each segment of music. For example, before the music begins, you ask the children to move like bears. They must then freeze like bears when the music stops. But before it starts again, you ask them to move next like raccoons, and so on.

FARM ANIMALS

LEARNING OBJECTIVES: To familiarize the children with farm animals and to foster greater respect for them.

This Little Piggy

Background Information. Talk to the children about pigs and their characteristics. You might discuss such common traits as their habit of rolling in the mud, their weight, the short legs that keep them low to the ground, their curly tails, and the sounds they make (snorts and grunts, as well as oinks). You can also mention that they eat side by side at a trough—and anything else you can think of.

Activity. Give the children a chance to briefly experiment with moving like pigs. (While doing so, they should keep the pigs' heaviness in mind.) Then, remaining ''in character,'' they move appropriately to the challenges you present. These challenges come in the form of the chant ''This little piggy . . . ,'' with the line completed by the following possibilities:

Rolled in the mud   Called to a friend

Ate dinner   Lay down

Went for a walk

Horseplay

Background Information. This activity provides an opportunity to introduce—or practice —the locomotor skill of galloping. Performed with an uneven rhythm, the gallop calls for one foot to lead, with the other playing ''catch-up.'' Although a child should learn to gallop with the dominant foot forward, he or she should eventually also learn to execute the gallop with the other foot forward.

Before introducing this skill, talk to the children about horses and how they move. Have the children ever seen horses? How do they look when they're running?

Activity.   Demonstrate galloping for those children who don't yet know how to gallop, helping those who need extra assistance by holding hands and galloping beside them. Naturally, not all of the children will master this skill the first day they try, so you should ask the children to perform the following by simply asking them to ''move like a horse does.'' Challenges include moving in the following ways:

Forward	In a zigzag path
In a circle	Occasionally leaping a fence
In a curving path	Stopping for a drink of water

Which Came First?

Background Information.   It's an age-old question: Which came first, the chicken or the egg? Though the children may not have an opinion when first asked, they just might after you've had a chance to discuss the dilemma with them.

Talk to them about where eggs (and chickens) come from, discussing the process of chickens laying eggs in a nest, the eggs hatching to reveal baby chicks, which then grow up to lay more eggs in other nests. Especially spend some time describing the hatching process, which involves the baby chick chipping away at the shell, little by little, from the inside of the egg. Finally, when enough of the shell has been removed, the baby chick is freed, but exhausted; so it's a while before the chick is able to get up and move around. (Some of your children may have witnessed this process before, as many country fairs and science museums have eggs hatching under sun lamps. But if there are children who've never seen this phenomenon, try to be as detailed as possible in your description. Or provide a picture book that shows the process.)

Also, discuss the characteristics of full-grown chickens with the children. What do chickens look like? How do they sound? How do they move? How do they eat?

Activity.   Ask the children to each pretend to be an egg in a nest. Then, as they imagine their nests getting warmer, they pretend to be baby chicks working their way out of the eggs.

They should continue with the process, just as you described it to them (you can narrate if you find it helpful), until they've finally grown to be adult chickens. At that time, they should be moving in the way full-grown chickens do, running around the barnyard, pecking at food on the ground, clucking, and laying more eggs!

"On the Farm"

Background Information.   The following poem is intended to familiarize the children with a variety of animals that might be found on a farm. Discuss the animals mentioned, remembering to talk with the children about the way each looks and moves.

Activity.   Ask the children to pretend to be each of the animals written about in the following poem:

Waddling is the duck's own way
Of moving on the ground;
But when she moves into water
There's no better swimmer found!

Gobble, gobble, the turkey says
As he surveys the land.
He has feathers that when spread out
Look very much like a fan!

The cow just loves to chew on grass,
Then take a casual stroll.
To stroll and chew and stroll and chew
Is her one and only goal!

Kids is the name for little goats,
And they just love to play.
Climbing, leaping, butting, jumping—
That is how they spend their day!

"Old MacDonald"

Background Information.   "Old MacDonald Had a Farm" is the perfect song for a farm-animal activity. The version presented here, however, is a variation on the traditional theme, offering an opportunity for problem solving as well as movement. But with the experience your children have had with animals to this point, they shouldn't have any trouble with the additional challenge.

Before beginning, review the animals (and their characteristics, if necessary) that might be found on a farm. Also remind the children that certain domestic animals (primarily cats and dogs) are also sometimes seen on farms.

Activity.   Instruct the children to each think of a farm animal they would like to be. You then begin to sing "Old MacDonald had a farm," and so on. When you get to the line, "And on his farm he had a _____," instead of singing the name of an animal, point to a child, who then imitates the actions of the animal he or she has chosen to be (without making any sounds). The rest of the children must guess what kind of animal is being imitated. Once they've guessed correctly, everyone sings the song, including the name of the animal and the appropriate sound. Continue until every child has had a chance to be an animal.

Note. Tell the group that if another child portrays an animal they've chosen, they can either select another animal or perhaps find a different way to portray the same one.

JUNGLE ANIMALS

LEARNING OBJECTIVES: To acquaint children with jungle animals and their environment; to alleviate any fears the children may harbor regarding the animals; to foster greater respect for these creatures and their environment.

The Elephant

Background Information. Chances are the children have all seen elephants—at least on TV. But spend some time, anyway, reviewing those physical and character traits that make an elephant what it is. Especially place some emphasis on the elephant's weight and therefore the heaviness of its movements.

Activity. Ask the children to imagine they're elephants and to show you the following:

An elephant walking
Ivory tusks
An elephant's tail swishing
An elephant eating (using trunk)
Big, floppy ears
An elephant showering (using trunk)
An elephant running
An elephant lying down

Monkey See, Monkey Do

Background Information.   This partner activity is a variation on the Mirror Game, in which one child performs movements and the other, facing the first, imitates those movements as though he or she were the first child's mirror reflection. It's an excellent exercise for teaching children to perform with their bodies what their eyes are seeing.

Talk to the children about mirrors and their reflections. Then talk to them about monkeys and their habit of imitating what they see. Have the children ever seen monkeys? What kinds of things do they do? (Possible answers here include scratching their heads, clapping, making "monkey" sounds, and jumping up and down.)

Activity.   Have the children pair off and face one another. Pretending to be a monkey, the first child in each pair performs a movement that a monkey might be seen doing (based, for the most part, on your discussion). The second child then imitates that movement. After a while, the children switch roles, so that both have a chance to be "leader."

"The Giraffe"

Background Information.   If possible, show the children a picture of a giraffe. Have the children ever seen a giraffe before? It's the tallest of all living animals! What's the giraffe's most striking feature? How do they think it would feel if a giraffe ever had a sore throat? Explain that giraffes eat leaves from the tops of trees in the jungle. (It must take a long time to swallow!) Also point out that the giraffe's front legs are longer than its back legs.

Activity.   The children act as giraffes to the accompaniment of the following poem:

> I am tall,
> As tall as can be;
> I can eat
> From the tops of trees!
>
> Gulp, gulp, gulp,
> I swallow my food,
> Then eat more
> If I'm in the mood!
>
> I can run
> With my tall front legs;
> They're so long
> They resemble pegs!
>
> I can bend,
> Though it takes a while;
> High to low
> Can feel like a mile!

"Hippos and Rhinos"

Background Information.   When I was a child, I was always getting hippos and rhinos confused—and I suspect that's the case with many children. Perhaps this activity can help clarify things in your students' minds.

   If at all possible, show the children pictures of both a hippopotamus and a rhinoceros. Then talk about the differences between the two. The most obvious difference, of course, is that the rhino has a horn protruding from its snout. The hippo, on the other hand, has large, protruding eyes, reminiscent of a bullfrog's. With regard to their movements, I tend to think of rhinos charging and hippos lumbering, or easing themselves into a body of water.

   Explain to the children that the "guy" used in the following poem is just an expression, assuring them that hippos and rhinos can also be "girls."

Activity.   The children act as rhinos and hippos, as appropriate, to the accompaniment of the following poem:

> *Hippopotamus* is a very strange name—
> It belongs to a guy with big eyes.
> And when he opens up his mouth,
> You can hardly believe its size!
>
> *Rhinoceros* is a very strange name—
> It belongs to a guy with a horn.
> And if he were not quite so short
> You'd think he was a unicorn!
>
> The hippo lumbers, and he likes to bathe;
> The rhino's been known to charge.
> And though they both are short and squat,
> They both are really rather large!
>
> But get them straight now in your mind,
> For they are not the same.
> The rhino is known for his horn;
> Big eyes and mouth the hippo's fame!

A Photo Safari

Background Information.   I like to think that when the children of today grow up, should they decide to go on safari, it will be to shoot photos of the animals and not the animals themselves. Their trophies will be albums and videotapes they can share with their friends, and not animal heads mounted on walls.

   Talk to the children about what a photo safari would be like— riding through the jungle in a jeep, witnessing all sorts of wild animals in their natural habitat, and capturing those sights forever on film. Also, if you're going to include in the activity any animals the children have not yet portrayed, discuss them with the children.

Activity. Explain to the children that you're going to pretend to be on a safari, spotting and photographing all kinds of jungle animals. They, in turn, will pretend to be the animals.

As you ready your ''camera,'' you call out the name of the animal you've spotted. The children then portray that animal. You can choose from the following:

Lions	Zebras
Hippos	Elephants
Apes	Gazelles
Giraffes	Rhinos
Tigers	Chimpanzees

chapter 7

The Sea

- ocean creatures
- the beach
- tides & storms & other stuff

OCEAN CREATURES

LEARNING OBJECTIVES: To familiarize the children with ocean creatures; to foster greater respect for these creatures and for their environment.

Follow That Fish!

Background Information.   Talk to the children about the different kinds of fish there are. What was the smallest fish they ever saw? The biggest? How do fish move? What are some different things fish do? (Possibilities include jumping out of the water, eating food from the ocean floor, flapping their fins, and flipping their tails.) Explain that fish often swim together in groups, called *schools*.

Activity.   Choose a child to begin as "lead fish." That child starts moving about the room, pretending to be a fish (and performing fishlike movements), with the other children following and imitating. Repeat this until every child has had a chance to lead.

Note. If you have a large group of children, you might choose to break them up into several "schools," so there are just a few fish following each leader.

Rhythmic Lobsters

Background Information.   For this activity, it would be perfect if every child had a pair of castinets. But that's probably not possible, so a little imagination will have to do as a substitute!

The idea behind the activity is for the children to pretend they're lobsters and to imagine their hands are lobster claws. Therefore, you'll want to talk to the children about what lobsters look like (especially their claws).

Activity.   This is a rhythm exercise. You clap out various groupings of beats, and the children repeat them, pretending to be lobsters. In other words, you will clap three times, for instance, at a moderate tempo. The children will repeat those three beats with their hands, which they're holding in the air and pretending are lobster claws. Simultaneous with the movement of their hands the children make clicking noises with their mouths (pretending their claws are making the clicks).

Note. You'll want to choose rhythm groupings according to the age and experience of your students. Generally speaking, the younger your children, the shorter and slower the rhythm groupings should be. For example, with very young children, you might clap out 1-2, with a pause between the one and the two. You then increase the challenge by clapping the same pattern at a faster tempo and, later, increasing the number of claps. With older children (or those with more experience with rhythms), you can even combine groupings. For example, you might clap 1-2, 1-2-3, with a slight pause between phrases.

"Somewhere Deep in the Ocean"

Background Information.   Talk to the children about each of the animals mentioned in the poem here: dolphins, whales, sharks, and seals. Discuss the creatures' physical and character traits and the differences between the ways each moves. Have the children ever seen any of these animals? What do they remember most about them?

Activity.   The following song is sung to the tune of "Somewhere Over the Rainbow." For each verse, the children pretend to be the animal being sung about.

>Somewhere deep in the ocean
>A dolphin plays.
>Swimming, splashing, and chatting—
>That's how she spends her days!
>
>Somewhere deep in the ocean
>Whales do live.
>They can be very graceful,
>Even though quite massive!
>
>Somewhere deep in the ocean
>A shark roams.
>It can be very scary
>To come upon his home!
>
>Somewhere deep in the ocean
>Swims a seal,
>Sliding throughout the blue sea
>Slippery as an eel!

The Jellyfish

Background Information.   A photo of a jellyfish would be most helpful. But even if you don't have one available, you can describe the jellyfish to your children by explaining that it's the shape of a flying saucer. Also, the jellyfish is known for its fluid movement— because it's of a consistency similar to jelly! How do the children think jelly moves? Is the movement tense or relaxed?

Activity.   Ask the children to each assume the shape of a jellyfish—at whatever level they prefer. Once they've done so, instruct them to relax various parts of their bodies, starting with the toes and moving up to the head. Then, once the children are completely relaxed, you tell them they feel just like a jellyfish does. Now, reminding them to continue feeling like a jellyfish, ask them to move in the way a jellyfish would.

<u>Note</u>. If you'd like to use this as a relaxation exercise, after the children have moved like jellyfish, ask the "jellyfish" to show you how they sleep.

The Eel

Background Information.   This is a group activity, requiring lots of cooperation. Impress that upon the children, making success a challenge and a goal for them.

Talk to the children about eels (provide a picture, if possible), explaining that eels are actually fish that look like snakes. The electric eel is one type; it can grow up to 6 feet long and has the ability to shock in the way that electricity does.

Activity.   Explain to the children that, together, they're going to form an eel—a very long eel—and they're going to pretend the eel is swimming in the ocean. The children begin by getting on the floor and moving individually, as they believe eels would. Then, at a signal from you, one by one, they start to join together by taking hold of another child's ankles—until all the children are joined and moving like a giant eel. Finally, when the children have successfully accomplished this, you tell them they've become an *electric* eel and you've just turned on their electricity! What would that look like?

<u>Note</u>. If you find the indiscriminate joining to be too confusing for the children, assign one child to take the ankles of another child nearby by calling out their names.

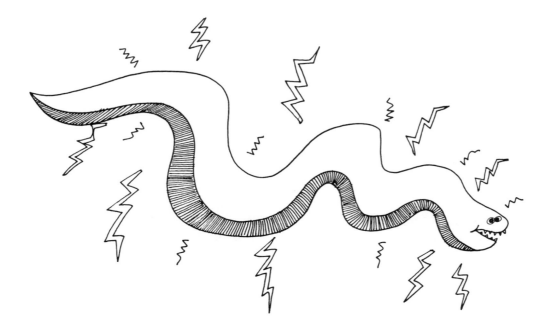

THE BEACH

Things at the Beach

Background Information. This activity provides an excellent opportunity for children to explore the concepts of space and shape—necessary preparation for abstract thought! Talk with the children about the things (alive and otherwise) that they see when they go to the beach. Can they describe the shapes of those things? Specifically discuss the shapes of the ideas listed here.

Activity. Ask the children to show you the shapes of the following and of those mentioned during your discussion.

Sailboats	Surfboards
Seashells	Radios
Starfish	Sand castles
Dogs	Picnic baskets
Crabs	Frisbees
Beachballs	Blankets!

Beach Activities

Background Information. Ask the children to tell you what kinds of activities they and other people participate in when they go to the beach.

Activity. Ask the children to show you what it looks like to perform certain beach activities. Possibilities include these:

Swim	Build castles in the sand
Jog	Play ''tag'' with the waves
Play volleyball	Read a book
Play with a Frisbee	Have a barbecue
Surf	Take a nap!

Sand Castles

Background Information. Talk to the children about castles and the various elements that *make* them castles (for instance, towers, moats, and drawbridges). Help them to form a very clear image of a castle in their minds. (If you have pictures available, they can certainly help.) Then talk a bit about building castles in the sand: what makes a good sand castle, how the sand must be wet in order to hold together, and so forth.

Activity. Tell the children you're going to build a sand castle, and *they're* going to be the sand. Start by having them each get into the smallest shape possible, pretending to be a tiny grain of sand (they should each be in their own "personal space"; that is, they shouldn't be close enough to touch each other). You then begin to gather the "grains of sand" together into a "lump," from which you'll shape your castle. Proceed to build the castle by having some children remain low to the floor—some in a circle, others forming the drawbridge. Then shape the castle itself by using the different levels in space. In other words, the castle will grow taller as some children are asked to kneel, others to crouch, to stand with bended knees, and to stand upright. Finally, a few children can pretend to be the flags waving at the top of the castle by standing on tiptoe, as tall as they can be, and imitating the movement of a flag in the breeze.

Walking on the Beach

Background Information. Ask the children to tell you some of the reasons a person might be walking along the beach: perhaps for exercise, looking for seashells, to be alone to think, to feel the cool sand or water on his or her feet, or to walk a dog.

Activity. Ask the children to show you how it would look to walk on the beach in the following ways:

On hot sand burning the feet	As though sad
With a dog on a leash	Briskly, for exercise
Through wet, sticky sand	Pulling a kite
Looking for shells	Bouncing a ball
As though cold	As though happy

Taking It Easy

Background Information. This is a great relaxation exercise, as well as an opportunity to stimulate imaginations. To enhance the mood, you might want to have soft music playing in the background. Many of the so-called New Age recordings consist of appropriate pieces for this activity, as do *Quiet Times* and *Classical Quiet Times* from *More Music for Moving & Learning* (Pica & Gardzina, 1990).

Talk to the children about some of the reasons people lie around on the beach (to get a tan, to relax, to take a nap, to read). What are some of the sensations experienced when lying on the beach? What might they feel (e.g., the warm sun, the cool breeze, the softness of a blanket on the sand)? What might they hear (e.g., the waves rolling in or lapping at the shore, seagulls calling)? What might they smell (the fresh sea air is one possibility)?

Activity.   Ask the children to lie on the floor, close their eyes, and imagine that they're lying on blankets at the beach. Then paint a picture in their minds for them, describing—in a quiet and soothing voice—the things they're feeling, hearing, and smelling.

TIDES AND STORMS AND OTHER STUFF

> **LEARNING OBJECTIVES:** To acquaint children with certain aspects of the sea not previously explored; to foster appreciation and respect for this important environment.

Sea Gulls

Background Information.   It is the herring gull that is commonly known as the "sea gull." Provide a picture if you can, and talk to the children about how sea gulls look, walk, and fly. Also discuss the other activities listed here.

Activity.   Stressing realism, ask the children to pretend to be sea gulls doing the following:

> Walking the beach
> Soaring through the sky
> Diving for fish
> Dropping a clamshell onto a rock
> Riding a wave

Note. Soothing music or a recording of ocean sounds can make this activity seem even more real to the children.

Rockin' the Boat

Background Information.   How many of the children have ever been out in a boat on the ocean? What was it like? What kind of boat were they in? Discuss the different kinds of boats that might be found on the ocean. Possibilities include sailboats, motorboats, cabin cruisers, even boats that are paddled or rowed. Then talk about the ocean itself— what it's like when it's calm and when it's windy and when there's a ferocious storm. Have the children ever seen the ocean during a storm, maybe on TV? It almost seems as though the ocean is very angry.

Activity.   Ask the children to each choose the kind of boat they'd like to have. Then describe a scene to them like the one here, which they'll act out. The scene is as follows:

It's a bright, sunny day, and you decide to take your boat out on the ocean. Off you go, into the sparkling blue water. For a while, the cruise is peaceful. There's a gentle breeze, and the relaxing roll of the waves rocks the boat as though it were a baby's cradle.

Then, as you get further out, you notice clouds beginning to roll in. The sky goes from blue to gray, and the ocean does the same. Suddenly the gentle breeze becomes a biting wind, and the clouds open up with a downpour of slashing, wind-driven rain. Waves crash into and over your boat, drenching you. You no longer feel like a baby being rocked, but like a salad being tossed!

And, then, just as suddenly as the storm began, it starts to abate. The winds die down, the sun appears from behind a cloud, and the waves grow smaller. Your boat moves steadily again as the ocean grows calm. The sunshine dries everything off, including your wet clothes. And once more you begin to enjoy the serenity of your surroundings.

Deep-Sea Diving

Background Information. Talk to the children about the many things that can be found beneath the surface of the ocean. What do they think is down there? Have they ever seen pictures? Emphasize the fact that there's a living *world* down there.

Activity.   In this exercise, you're going to pretend to be the diver, and the children are going to be all the things you see as you explore the underwater world. Explain this to the children and then "don" your scuba gear! Some of the things you might spot include the following:

A fish	A shark
An octopus	Barnacles
A sponge	A jellyfish
The bubbles from your breathing	A crab
A sunken boat	An eel
A sea anemone (plant)	Another diver!

The Tide

Background Information.   Tides occur twice a day and are caused by the unequal gravitational pull of the sun and the moon on different parts of the earth. That, of course, is a fairly technical explanation for young children. But you can talk about high and low tides with the children and the fact that they're affected by the sun and the moon. Also discuss what waves look like from the beach during high and low tides. At high tide, waves tend to be larger—roaring in, cresting, and foaming as they approach the beach. During low tide, the waves not only don't come in as far, but they're smaller, rolling in more gently, with just some bubbles as they reach the sand.

Activity.   Ask the children to each move like a wave at low tide. Next, they pretend that time is passing and the tide is getting higher. The waves continue to grow until, finally, at high tide, they're as big as they get.

Note. If time permits, you can reverse this process. Or you can begin with high tide instead.

Alternate Activity.   Once your children have had the experience of acting as waves individually, you might want to try a group activity. For this, you would divide the children into rows, one behind the other. The "waves" then work together to depict low and high tides.

Bodies of Water

Background Information.   Do the children know how rivers, lakes, and bays differ from each other and from the ocean? Discuss these bodies of water with them, pointing out as many characteristics as you can. For instance, rivers flow. And, while a lake and bay could conceivably be the same size, a bay, which is salt water, is subject to tides, while a lake, which is fresh water, is not. Therefore, a lake has less motion to it. Also, a bay is smaller than the ocean. Finally, explain the ways in which these bodies of water can be connected.

Activity. Ask the children to choose what they would each like to pretend to be: a river, a lake, a bay, or an ocean. Then tell them you know a place where a river runs into and out of a small lake. Once it comes out of the lake, it eventually runs into a bay, and the bay is "around the corner" from the ocean. Can they show you what all that would look like? (It'll take some time and a lot of cooperation, but with some encouragement, they can do it!)

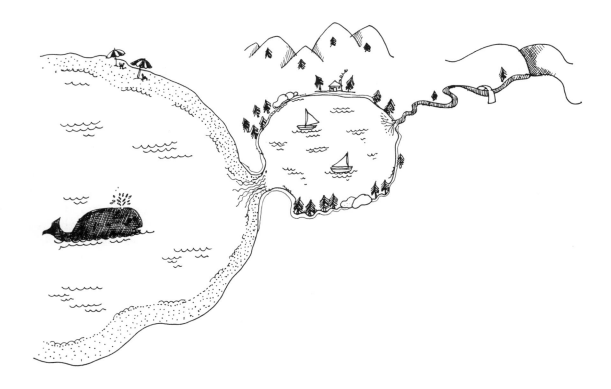

chapter
8

OCCUPATIONS

➪ keeping house
➪ wearing uniforms
➪ the Arts
➪ more professions

KEEPING HOUSE

LEARNING OBJECTIVES: To foster appreciation and respect for the occupation of homemaking; to help eliminate gender stereotyping where homemaking is concerned.

Washing

Background Information.   Talk to the children about how hard a job it is to be a home-maker—and how keeping things washed and clean is just a part of the job. Then ask them to tell you some of the things that need to be washed in a house.

Activity.   Ask the children to show you the movements involved in washing the following:

Windows	The dog
Dishes	The bathtub
The floor	A sink

Note. Be sure to stress realism. In other words, although the hand and arm movements involved in washing dishes may be similar to those required in washing a dog, the latter would occur at a lower level in space. Similarly, washing dishes also calls for rinsing and the careful placement of those dishes in a drainer.

"Preparing Meals"

Background Information.   Talk with the children about all the steps involved in preparing different kinds of meals. Some meals require chopping and stirring; others call for mixing and pouring (pancakes, for instance, must be mixed, poured, and then flipped). Some foods are cooked in pans on the stove, others baked in the oven; some, like salad, don't require actual cooking at all. Some dishes have complicated menus that must be followed exactly, while others can be made from memory or experimentation!

Activity.   The children sing the following song with you (to the tune of "Here We Go 'Round the Mulberry Bush") while performing the action described. What others can they think of?

> First we have to chop the food,
> Chop the food, chop the food.
> First we have to chop the food
> So we can eat our dinner.
>
> Now we have to mix it up,
> Mix it up, mix it up.
> Yes, we have to mix it up
> So we can eat our dinner.

Now we have to pour the food,
Pour the food, pour the food.
Now we have to pour the food
So we can eat our dinner.

Finally, we serve the food,
Serve the food, serve the food.
Finally, we serve the food
And now we eat our dinner!

Taking Care of Clothes

Background Information.   Clothes require a lot of care if they're going to remain clean and nice-looking. Some of the steps involved in taking care of clothes are washing them (some by hand but most in the washing machine), drying them (on a line or in a dryer), ironing them, folding and putting them in drawers, or hanging them in closets.

Activity.   Separate the children into groups of four and ask each group to form a line, side by side. The first child in each line acts out washing the clothes; the second dries them; the third irons; and the fourth puts them away. Each child chooses how to perform his or her task. After each of the four tasks is completed, the group rotates, with the last child going to the beginning of the line.

Alternate Activity.   Once the children are familiar with this activity, you might want to introduce the musical elements of *accelerando* and *ritardando* into it. You can do this by setting a beginning tempo with hand-clapping at a medium slow pace. After every eighth clap, call out the word *change* or *switch* or *next* (or the name of the next task). Then, after each time through the line, you increase the tempo of your clapping. When the children's actions have become as fast as you want them to get, reverse the process, decreasing the tempo until you're back to where you started.

A Dusting Dance

Background Information.   Keeping a house dust-free is not an easy job, since all kinds of things, from woodstoves and fireplaces to opening and closing the doors, tend to create dust. And doing the dusting itself can be bothersome because the dust can get in eyes and make them water or get in noses, causing sneezes. Also, there are so many things that have to be dusted. Some of them are way down low, and some of them are way up high. Some of them are tiny objects, like knickknacks, which have to be lifted and dusted under.

Activity.   Provide each child with a piece of cloth and explain that they're going to turn dusting into a *fun* job by doing a dusting "dance." Put on a piece of lively instrumental music (Mozart's *Eine Kleine Nacht Musik*, a Strauss waltz, or a Top 40 favorite, for example) and invite the children to "dust and dance," using their props in any way they like.

Note. If necessary, to encourage creative use of space, remind children that they have a whole house to dust and that bending and stretching are required to reach everything. Is the dust tickling their noses? Are they using all the parts of their cloths? Of course, realism isn't as important here as fun and creativity. And you can make this activity even more fun by asking what other body parts they can hold their dust cloths with!

Household Machines

Background Information. In the "olden days," homemakers didn't have many machines to make their jobs easier. But in modern times there are more and more machines being invented to help homemakers. Ask the children to name some of the machines in their households. How do they work?

Activity. Ask the children to pretend to be each of the following:

Washing machine	Electric can opener
Dryer	Blender
Vacuum cleaner	Dishwasher

Alternate Activity. Tell the children they're going to create a brand new machine, one never seen before. What job do they think it should do? What would they like to call it?

Begin by having one child repeatedly perform a movement that can be executed in one spot (such as jumping lightly in place or standing and reaching alternate arms toward the ceiling). A second child then stands near the first and contributes a second movement that relates in some way to the first. For example, if the first child is performing an up-down motion by bending and stretching, the second child might choose to do the reverse, standing beside his or her classmate. A third child might choose an arm or leg motion that's timed to move between the two bodies bending and stretching. As these movements continue, each remaining student adds a functioning part to the machine. They may choose any movements at all, as long as they don't interfere with the actions of others and they contribute in some way to the machine. (You can even ask the children to perform sounds to accompany their motions!)

WEARING UNIFORMS

The Nurse

Background Information.   Have any of your children ever been in the hospital? If so, can they tell the rest of the group about the nurses? What kinds of things did they do?

Talk to the children about nurses and how indispensible they are. Especially discuss the responsibilities cited below. If necessary, explain that both men and women can be nurses.

Activity.   Ask the children to act out the following duties, pretending they're nurses:

Fluffing up a patient's pillows
Taking a temperature; reading the results
Giving a shot
Bringing a patient's meal
Listening to a heartbeat with a stethoscope
Writing information on a patient's chart
Dispensing medication
Taking a pulse

"The Mail Carrier"

Background Information.   Delivering mail to the correct addresses is an especially important job. Just think of what would happen if bills and letters from friends and loved ones were delivered to the wrong people or never delivered at all! For instance, what if a child sent his or her grandmother a birthday card but she never got it! Grandma might feel forgotten and unloved!

Activity.   Read the following poem once through to the children. Then simply ask them to pretend to be mail carriers as you read the poem again.

> The mail carrier totes the shoulder bag
> With pride and care, because
> Getting mail to its destination
> Is the important work he does.

Driving the truck to the end of the street,
Then walking down one side;
Stopping at every mailbox there is
To deposit the mail inside.

She continues in this very same way,
Whistling a happy tune,
Pausing to say a friendly "hello"
And a pleasant "good afternoon."

So now the mail has all been delivered
To where it ought to be.
The sender can be sure of the mail
And so, too, can the addressee!

The Firefighter

Background Information.   Firefighting is an occupation that's particularly fascinating to children. To a child, the firefighter is—with good reason—a hero.

   Talk to your group about all the things firefighters do. Do any of your children want to be firefighters? Why?

Activity.   Ask the children to act out the following duties, pretending to be firefighters.

Slide down the pole
Run to the fire truck
Hold on tightly as the truck races to the fire
Get out the fire hose
Hose down the burning building
Chop through a wall with an ax
Climb the ladder
Return the equipment to the truck

Alternate Activity.   You can also have the children pretend to be the all-important fire-fighting equipment. Ask them to depict the following:

The fire pole
A fire truck
The ladder being extended
The fire hose being unraveled
The fire hose gushing water
An ax breaking down a wall
The ladder being lowered

"Waiting Tables"

Background Information.   Unlike nurses and firefighters, waiters and waitresses are not in the business of saving lives. But a good waitperson is a valuable commodity, adding cheer to a diner's day and making a good meal even better. Talk to your children about the tasks involved in waiting tables—and how important it is to do good work, *whatever* the job.

Activity.   Teach your children the song here, sung to the tune of "This Old Man." Then ask them to sing it, as they each go about the business of pretending to be a waitperson. The children can act out any appropriate tasks they choose, based on your discussion. If they get stuck, you can offer reminders. Possibilities include these:

> Taking the orders
> Carrying a heavy tray
> Lowering the tray carefully onto a stand
> Serving the meals
> Pouring water or coffee
> Removing the empty plates

The lyrics of the song are as follows:

> Waiting tables
> Is what I do;
> I will bring your meal to you.
> With care and grace and a nice smile, too,
> I will do my best for you.

"The Bell Captain"

Background Information.   People who stay in hotels would often be lost (sometimes literally!) without the valuable assistance of a bell captain. Four of the bell captain's responsibilities are named in the little verse here. Talk to the children about these responsibilities and why they're so helpful to hotel guests.

Activity.   Ask the children to individually decide what action they'd like to perform—*in place*—for each of the lines in the following verse. When ready, the children stand in a row, side by side. You then continuously recite the verse—slowly at first—with each child in turn performing an action for the line being read. (You can go back and forth, moving down and up the line, or start again at the beginning of the line each time.) Gradually increase the pace until it's as fast as the children can handle. The verse is as follows:

> Open a door;
> Hail a cab.
> Give directions;
> Carry a bag.

Alternate Activity. As another activity, you can ask the children to form a circle and start walking slowly around. You then begin reciting the verse at a slow tempo, with the entire group performing every line together. Again, gradually increase the tempo.

THE ARTS

LEARNING OBJECTIVES: To foster appreciation for the contributions of visual and performing artists; to help the children see the arts as an option when making career choices.

The Sculptor

Background Information.   A sculptor is an artist who carves, molds, or shapes statues or figures from different materials. Sometimes the material is as hard as marble, which must be chiseled; sometimes it is as soft as clay, which must be molded.

   If there is a well-known sculpture in your area, use it as an example for the children, helping them to understand that before the sculpture could exist, an artist known as a *sculptor* had to imagine, design, and create it. Also talk to them specifically about molding clay into a sculpture. Most of them have probably worked with clay and can describe what it's like.

Activity.   Divide the children into pairs, and explain that one child is to be the sculptor and the other the clay. The ''clay'' starts as a lump on the floor. The ''sculptor'' then begins ''working the clay'' (by arranging limbs and body parts), creating whatever final shape is desired. Once the task is complete, the children reverse roles.

Note. Stress that the sculptor must work *gently* with the clay, and that certain body parts and limbs can only move in certain directions.

The Musician

Background Information.   Imagine a world without music! How sad a place the world would be if there were no music to listen and dance to.

What kinds of music do the children like best? Why? Talk to them—briefly—about the instruments used to make different styles of music. For example, a rock band generally consists of singers, guitars, bass guitar, and drums. A "big band" includes those same instruments, as well as horns (saxophones, clarinets, trumpets, and trombones). An orchestra wouldn't be an orchestra without a piano, strings (violins, violas, and cellos), French horns, flutes, tubas, and percussion instruments (cymbals, gong, triangle, etc.). If the children were musicians, what instruments would they want to play?

Activity.   Ask the children to pretend to be playing the following instruments:

Guitar	Violin
Piano	Triangle
Drums	Cymbals
Flute	Trumpet
Slide trombone	Gong
Saxophone	

Alternate Activity.   Divide the children into groups of four or five and ask each group to form a "rock and roll band." Compulsory instruments are guitar, bass guitar, and drums. Optional elements are saxophone player, keyboard player, and lead singer (although it's necessary to have at least one singer, instrumentalists can also act as singers).

Another option is to create a "big band" or "orchestra" with your entire group.

The Puppeteer

Background Information.   A puppeteer is someone who entertains with puppets—most often for children. In my youth we had Shari Lewis and her Lamb Chop. The last and present generations of children have the creations of the late, great Jim Henson to identify with. Among these famous puppets are Kermit the Frog, Miss Piggy, Oscar the Grouch, and Big Bird.

Talk to the children about puppets, explaining the difference between hand puppets and marionettes, which are puppets operated from above by strings or wires (and sometimes by a rod). Have the children ever seen a puppet show in person? What kinds of puppets were in it?

Activity.   Divide the children into pairs. One child is to be the puppeteer and the other a puppet.

The "puppet" should sit on the floor in front of the "puppeteer." It's then up to the latter to "give life" to her or his puppet. Each puppeteer can decide what kind of puppet to operate and what kinds of movements that puppet will perform. After a while, the partners reverse roles.

The Dancer

Background Information. Talk to the children in general terms about different kinds of professional dancing. Ballet, for instance, is a very old form of dance that is extremely structured and graceful. Tap dancing involves tapping out rhythms with the feet and requires tap shoes, which have little pieces of metal on the tips, toes, and heels that make the tapping sounds. Jazz dancing is also very rhythmic but involves the whole body, including the head, shoulders, and hips. Much of the dancing seen in upbeat music videos can be considered jazz dance.

Because dance has suffered from gender stereotyping, it would be helpful if you discussed the role of the male in professional dance. Of course, if the children watch music videos, they *see* men dancing. But you can also point out that, although both male and female ballet dancers must be very strong in order to execute the difficult steps, male ballet dancers must be *especially* strong to lift their female partners off the floor. Also, most famous tap dancers have been men.

Activity. Ask the children to pretend that they're wearing tap shoes and to make up a tap dance. Then put on a piece of slow, classical music and ask the children to pretend to be ballet dancers. Finally, put on a Top 40 number and ask the children to pretend to be dancing in a music video.

Note. Because the children are *pretending* to be dancers—and are not simply being asked to dance to the music—they shouldn't be any more self-conscious than when asked to pretend to be mail carriers, for instance. However, if you find that dancing still makes them uncomfortable, make a game of Statues (see p. 56) out of the activity.

"An Artist's Life"

Background Information.   So far the children have acted out the roles of sculptor, musician, puppeteer, and dancer. But there are other professions that fall into the category of the arts, including the work of poets, writers, photographers, conductors, painters, actors, choreographers, and composers. The poem here deals with four of these.

   Talk to your children about all of the artists mentioned, focusing particularly on writers, conductors, painters, and actors.

Activity.   Read the poem here in its entirety. Then ask the children to act out the verses as you read it more slowly a second time. As you recite the last verse, the children can pretend to be any artists they choose—even those not mentioned in the poem.

> The writer sits with pen in hand
> Putting words upon the pages,
> Describing things that touch the heart
> Of readers through the ages.
>
> The conductor works with baton
> Weaving patterns in the air,
> Guiding musicians as they play
> With both subtlety and flair.
>
> The painter works in a studio
> Using colors dark and bright,
> Putting brush to canvas until
> The images are just right.
>
> The actor steps upon the stage
> And begins to play a role;
> The character requires all
> Of the body, heart, and soul.
>
> An artist's life is not easy,
> But it can be lived with pride.
> The work is done out of love so
> The artist is satisfied.

MORE PROFESSIONS

LEARNING OBJECTIVES: To call attention to and foster appreciation for a variety of jobs not previously covered; to emphasize the importance of doing a job well.

The Building Trades

Background Information. Without the building trades, we'd have no buildings or houses! Talk to the children about the roles of architects, carpenters, roofers, bricklayers, and painters, stressing the importance of doing good work. After all, if a building isn't well designed or constructed, it won't last very long, and people could even get hurt! (Although there are certainly others in the building trades, this activity focuses on some the children can most easily relate to.)

Activity. Ask the children to pretend to do the following tasks:

Design a house (on imaginary paper)
Carry two-by-fours
Hammer nails
Saw wood
Measure something
Check to see if a door is level
Carry shingles up a ladder
Lay bricks for a chimney
Paint the inside walls with a roller
Paint the inside trim with a brush
Paint the outside walls with a spray gun

"The Teacher"

Background Information. Teachers have one of the most important responsibilities in the world: to teach! They help people (children mostly) learn everything from the ABCs to algebra, from physical fitness to physics, from history to how to get along with others. Just about everything there is to know can be learned from a teacher.

Do any of the children in your group want to be teachers? What do they want to teach? Why?

Activity. Before acting out the following poem, ask the children to decide what movement they each want to perform for the last two lines of the first and last verses. Then, as you read the poem slowly, the children perform the appropriate movements. The poem is as follows:

> Writing on a blackboard,
> Reading from a book,
> Being sure that not one fact
> Has been overlooked.
>
> Working the computer,
> Pointing at the map,
> Blowing on the whistle when
> It's time to run a lap.
>
> Handing out assignments,
> Putting grades on tests;
> If someone has learned today,
> Teacher will feel blessed.

The Secretary

Background Information. Offices all over the world would cease to function if secretaries decided to stop working. Among the valuable services they perform for their employers are typing, answering the telephone, making appointments, greeting clients, taking dictation, and filing.

Talk to your children about each of these tasks. If you like, you can mention that, although most secretaries are women, many men also choose secretarial work as a profession.

Activity. Ask the children to pretend to do the following tasks, pretending to be secretaries:

Answer the telephone; make a call
Take dictation
Type a letter
Check the appointment book; make a notation in it
Show a client into the boss's office
Look up a telephone number in the phone book
File folders in the filing cabinet
Straighten up her or his desk

Alternate Activity. As with the firefighting activity, the children can also pretend to be the *tools* found in an office. Ask them to depict the following:

A typewriter
A pencil; a pencil writing

A telephone
A filing cabinet; a filing cabinet drawer sliding open and shut
A phone book; the phone book pages being flipped
A computer
The water cooler

The Mechanic

Background Information.   In the days before the automobile was invented, there was no such thing as an auto mechanic. But today people would be lost without their vehicles and, because vehicles break down, they would also be lost without mechanics. Not only is the mechanic's work important because we need our cars, but we also need to be *safe* in those cars. And if a mechanic doesn't do good work and something goes wrong with a vehicle, the people in it could be in danger!

Ask the children to name some of the jobs mechanics do. Then talk specifically with them about the jobs listed here.

Activity.   Ask the children to pretend to do the following:

Lift the hood of a car	Put air in the tires
Check the oil	Tow a car
Test the blinkers and lights	Do a tuneup
Test the horn	Wash the windshield
Pump gas	Test-drive a car
Change a tire	

<u>Note</u>. Doing the "tuneup" is wide open to individual interpretation. The responses ought to be interesting!

The Bank Teller

Background Information.   Despite the presence of automated teller machines, we still need *real* bank tellers to make transactions for us—and to add a personal, friendly touch to those transactions.

Have the children ever been in a bank? Do they know what a teller is? Do they know what he or she does? Do they know what a *bank* is for? After receiving their input (you'll probably get some wonderful responses to these questions), in the simplest of terms, explain deposits and withdrawals to them.

Activity.   This activity is based on the classic game Mother, May I? But it had to become a bit more complicated to go along with the topic.

Ask the children to stand in a row, facing you, at the far end of the room (the "vault"). You're going to be the "teller," and the children are going to represent the money. You will either "withdraw" from or make "deposits" to the vault. If you specify a withdrawal, the children will move forward (toward you); if you specify a deposit, the children will move backward. But there's more: In this game, you won't ask for baby steps or giant steps and so forth. You're going to withdraw and deposit *dollars* and *cents*, and the amounts will be represented by specific locomotor movements. A single cent is a step; a dollar is a jump; and $100 is a hop. (For example, if you say you need to withdraw 10 cents, the children will take 10 *steps* toward you. If you say you're depositing $4, the children will take 4 *jumps backward*. And if you say you're withdrawing or depositing $500, the children will take 5 *hops* forward or backward.) And, of course, before the children can move at all, they must ask, "Teller, may I?"

chapter 9

Transportation

flying the skies
riding the waves
driving, riding & cycling

"have boat ⛵,
wheels ⊚ or wings ✈
will travel!!"

FLYING THE SKIES

LEARNING OBJECTIVES: To familiarize children with various methods of traveling the skies.

Airplane

Background Information. When you think about flying the skies, you generally tend to think about airplanes first. But airplanes come in different sizes and shapes and therefore possess different characteristics. The Concorde, for instance, is the fastest jet in the world. A glider plane, on the other hand, has no engine, so it's quite a bit slower; it's also quieter and more graceful than the Concorde. A large cargo plane is neither quick nor graceful nor quiet; in fact, the cargo probably gets a rather bumpy, noisy ride.

Discuss all this with the children. Also talk about the basics of taxiing into position for takeoff, gaining speed on the runway, taking off, climbing to cruising altitude, leveling-off, descending, landing, and taxiing to the arrival gate.

Activity. Ask the children to pretend to be the following:

A cargo plane
The Concorde
A glider plane

Then ask them to pretend to be a passenger jet and to do the following:

Taxi out from the gate and into position
Accelerate down the runway
Take off
Climb to cruising altitude
Level off and continue toward the passengers' destination
Descend
Land
Taxi to the gate

Blast Off

Background Information. For as long as there have been ''spaceships,'' children have been fascinated with them. Talk to your children about the exploration of space—that shuttle craft are launched, both with and without astronauts, to do things like take pictures of the earth and other planets. We learn a lot about our solar system that way.

Have the children ever watched a space launch on television? Talk to them about the countdown, the ignition of the shuttle boosters, the lift-off, and the landing. Then discuss the things an astronaut might see while traveling through the sky, and the element of weightlessness.

Activity. Ask the children to each pretend to be a spaceship on the launching pad. Then, with as much drama as possible, count down from 10. The "spaceships" then blast off and begin their ascent into outer space. Once "in orbit," the children can pretend instead to be the astronauts. What are they doing inside the spaceship? What are they seeing while on their journey?

The spaceships should then be put into a "holding pattern" while the astronauts venture out. After moving about weightlessly for a while, the astronauts return to their spaceships and bring them back to earth, landing them safely on the runway.

Up, Up, and Away

Background Information. Have the children ever seen a hot air balloon? (They have if they've seen *The Wizard of Oz!*) Show them a picture if you can, and talk about the basket where the people stand and the large, brightly colored balloon in the shape of a light bulb.

The balloon must first be laid out flat on the ground, and a fan is used to open it up. It then takes about five people to get it upright. Once upright, a fire is lit (the balloons use propane gas), and the fire creates the hot air that gets the balloon going. A hole in the top of the balloon is then made larger or smaller to regulate speed and direction. Hot air balloons can only be launched on days when it is not too windy.

Activity. Ask the children to lie on the floor, each pretending to be a hot air balloon lying flat on the ground. Tell them that a fan has started to blow, and they are slowly expanding (while still lying down). Once fully expanded, the hot air balloons are lifted upright and the fires started. The balloons then rise slowly into the air, where they drift smoothly over the trees.

After a while, reverse the entire process.

Whirlybird

Background Information. *Whirlybird* is a nickname for the helicopter. Have the children ever seen one? Show a picture if you can, or describe a helicopter to them. Sometimes the front is a glass bubble that surrounds the pilot. It sits on two long runners that resemble skis. The propellers are on top and spin horizontally (rather than vertically, as on the wings of a plane), beginning slowly and gradually increasing speed as the helicopter prepares for takeoff. The tail is long and reminiscent of a dragonfly.

Unlike a plane, a helicopter doesn't need to take off down a runway, because it lifts straight off the ground. It also has the ability to hover (since *hovering* is critical to the activity, discuss this concept with your children), and the ride is "bumpier" in a helicopter than in a plane.

Activity. This activity will provide the children with experience in the element of bound (interrupted) flow.

Begin by asking the children to imagine they're helicopters preparing for takeoff. Once the "helicopters" are airborne and moving about the "sky" (if necessary, remind the children that this is a bumpy ride), you will occasionally (at random intervals) call out "Hover!" The helicopters must then do exactly that—until you call out "Proceed!"

Note. Vary the amount of time between commands and keep the children guessing as to when they'll come!

Alternate Activity.   You can also explore the element of shape by dividing your class into groups of at least three and asking each group to create the shape of a helicopter, including runners, body, propellers, and tail.

"The Air Show"

Background Information.   At air shows, stunt pilots in special jet planes amaze their audiences with all kinds of daredevil maneuvers. Talk to the children about the maneuvers cited in the following poem.
   Has anyone in your group ever seen an air show? What was it like?

Activity.   Ask the children to act out the following poem, each pretending to be a stunt pilot's plane.

Rising, rising into the sky,
Into the face of the sun—
Higher and higher and higher we fly,
The airplane and pilot as one.

Suddenly we turn upside down,
Flying backward through the air—
Now the nose is heading back toward the ground
As we make loopdy-loops with flair.

Leveling out, then rising once more,
Then cut the engine to dive—
Getting close enough to hear the crowd roar
As the engine sputters alive.

We rise and fall and rise again;
There's no other way to fly—
We dip and soar and fall into a spin,
Then speed away across the sky.

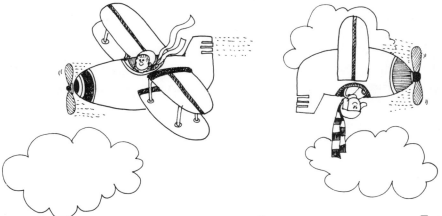

RIDING THE WAVES

LEARNING OBJECTIVES: To familiarize children with various methods of water travel; to heighten awareness of the earth's water as a valuable resource.

Canoeing

Background Information.   Have your children ever seen a canoe? Do they know how a canoe is paddled? Talk to them about canoeing and what it would be like in both smooth and rough water. Describe *white-water rapids* to them as part of a river where the water moves very quickly (making it frothy and white) and the surface is usually broken by obstructions, like rocks. To *shoot the rapids* in a canoe means to maneuver the boat through the rough water.

Activity.   This is a partner activity (two people per canoe) that calls for cooperation.

Ask the children to take partners, who stand, one behind the other, facing the same direction and pretend to share a single canoe. The forward child leads in terms of dictating the direction of movement. Otherwise, the following instructions can lend themselves to individual interpretation. And it isn't necessary for partners to always be "paddling" on the same side of the canoe.

Ask the partners to pretend to do the following:

> Carry the canoe to the edge of the water
> Get the canoe into the water
> Get into the canoe without tipping it over
> Paddle around a lake
> Paddle against a sudden, strong wind
> Go fishing while the canoe drifts along
> Shoot the rapids

The Submarine

Background Information.   A submarine, which spends more time underwater than "riding the waves," is a form of water transportation for members of the military and oceanographers. By definition, a submarine is a "submersible ship."

Talk to the children about subs, showing a picture if possible. Describe the functions of the periscope and hatch, and talk about the commands listed here. This activity will not only call attention to submarines as a form of water transportation, but will also focus on the concepts of *up* and *down*.

Activity. Ask the children to pretend to be submarines, moving along the surface of the ocean. You are the commander, and as they travel about the ocean, they are to do as you command. The commands you can issue include the following:

Dive! (Submerge and continue travel underwater)

Up periscope! (Once up, the periscope should swivel around in all directions)

Down periscope!

Surface! (Rise to the ocean's surface)

Open hatch! (This and the following command can only be issued when the sub is above water)

Close hatch!

"Row, Row, Row Your Boat"

Background Information. "Row, Row, Row Your Boat" is a classic song typically sung in *rounds*. One person or group begins singing; at the conclusion of the first line, the second person or group joins in, beginning with the first line. With this song, since there are only four lines, there can be only four rounds (individuals or groups). Explain this to the children. Also discuss the movement involved in rowing a boat, which is different from, say, paddling a canoe.

Activity. Divide your children into four groups and practice singing "Row, Row, Row Your Boat" in rounds. The lyrics are as follows:

> Row, row, row your boat
> Gently down the stream.
> Merrily, merrily, merrily, merrily,
> Life is but a dream.

Once the children are comfortable with the rounds, it's time to add movement to the song. Line the groups up at the end of the room, one behind the other, with the members of each group standing side by side (with enough elbow room for "rowing"). As the first group begins to sing, they start walking toward the other side of the room, making a rowing motion with their arms. The second group does likewise at the conclusion of the first line, and so on. When each group reaches the end of the room, the members can split up, half going to the right and half to the left, continuing the activity down the sides of the room. They can then meet in the middle and continue once more.

Alternate Activity. If you have the space—and enough carpet squares to go around— you can exercise the children's legs at the same time that you familiarize them with rowing and rounds. Instead of standing and walking across the room, the children can sit on carpet squares—still singing and performing the rowing motion, but using their feet and legs to propel themselves forward.

Boating

Background Information. This activity gives children the opportunity to experience the difference between pretending to *be* something and pretending to *do* something. Discuss the topics listed below, as well as the relationships between each *being* and *doing* pair. Also, show the children any pictures you have that can help make these images clearer.

   A kayak is a canvas-covered portable canoe. A double-bladed kayak paddle has a paddle on each end of the pole and is usually dipped alternately on either side of the boat.

Activity. Ask the children to pretend to *be* and *do* the following. To fully experience the contrast, you should alternate from one column to the other (it doesn't matter which you do first). But if you prefer, you can complete all of one column before doing the other.

Being	*Doing*
An anchor being raised	Raising an anchor
An outboard motor	Starting an outboard motor
The mast of a tall ship	Climbing the mast of a tall ship
A double-bladed kayak paddle	Paddling a kayak
A life preserver	Throwing out a life preserver
A rubber boat being inflated	Inflating a rubber boat

"Smooth Sailing"

Background Information. This activity lends itself to relaxation, as does the act of sailing itself. Have any of your children ever been out in a sailboat? Did they find it peaceful? Talk about the terms and images in the following poem.

Activity. Tell the children that they're to pretend to be the *sails* on a sailboat as you read the following poem, slowly and softly. They begin by lying "furled" upon the "deck."

> Starting now to unfurl,
> Rising slowly up the mast;
> Stretching, stretching,
> Open and free at last.
>
> Gently pushed by the wind,
> Billowing softly in the breeze;
> Sailing, sailing
> Over the peaceful seas.
>
> Swinging right, swinging left,
> Then heading back toward the shore;
> Falling, falling,
> Lying on deck once more.

DRIVING, RIDING, AND CYCLING

LEARNING OBJECTIVES: To familiarize the children with other types of transportation.

Traffic Lights

Background Information. Safety, of course, is an important issue where transportation—particularly driving—is concerned. Talk to your children about traffic lights. A red light means traffic must come to a stop, and a green light means drivers can go through an intersection. A yellow light means to proceed with caution, for a red light is about to appear.

For this activity, you'll need three large pieces of paper or cardboard—one red, one green, one yellow.

Activity. Explain to the children that they're to pretend they're driving cars or trucks. When they see a "green light" (you hold up the green paper), they can go. Similarly, a "red light" means they must stop. At the "yellow light" they should walk in place.

Alternate Activity. You can use this activity as an opportunity to practice any loco-motor skills. For example, a green light can indicate the children should *skip*. A yellow light can mean they must hop in place. Or, with the yellow light, you might substitute a *nonlocomotor* skill, such as twisting or shaking.

Bus Stop

Background Information. Have your children ever ridden a bus? If so, they know that buses—school buses and city buses—make frequent stops to let some passengers off and to pick up others. But the drivers don't stop just anywhere. There are designated *bus stops* along a route where people can get off and on.

Activity. Designate three or four "bus stops" in your room, and divide your group among them. Also determine where the bus "terminal" is, as that will be the spot where the "bus" begins and ends it daily route.

Acting as the driver, you begin your route by pausing at each of the bus stops to pick up passengers (the children get in line behind you). On your first trip around, all of the "passengers" should get on board. However, as you continue to make the rounds, passengers can get off and board the bus as they choose. When making your final round, all of the passengers should be deposited at their original stops before you return to the terminal.

Note. As you operate the "bus," you should remember that sometimes buses go fast and sometimes slow. Sometimes they come to red lights (come to a full stop), and some-times they get stuck in traffic (you can walk in place).

The first time you perform this activity, you should act as the bus driver. However, if you repeat it, you can let the children take turns being the driver.

"Cycling"

Background Information.   The bicycle is a nice, inexpensive, pollution-free way of getting around. How many of your children have bicycles? What's the farthest they've ever ridden?

Activity.   Teach the children the following song, sung to the tune of "A Bicycle Built for Two" (or "Daisy"). They can then sing it with you (or you can sing it to them) as they pretend to be cycling.

> Riding, riding
> On my brand new bike.
> The carefree feel of gliding
> Is what I especially like.
> I can pump up hills;
> I can coast down, too.
> I can ride without spills
> 'Cause I know just what to do.

Alternate Activity.   You can also ask your children to show you the differences involved in riding the following:

A tricycle

A unicycle

A mountain bike

A racing bike

A tandem bike (built for two)

A moped

All Aboard!

Background Information.   Children today haven't had as much opportunity to experience trains as some of us had. Have *any* of your children ridden a train? What was it like? Have they ever read (or heard) *The Little Engine That Could*? What was the longest train they ever saw?

The following is another Follow the Leader activity, but it requires more cooperation among the children than Bus Stop does.

Activity.   Ask the children to take partners, with each pair pretending to be a two-car train (the child in back should grasp the waist of the child in front). Then explain that as the trains travel about, being careful not to collide with one another, they should begin hooking on to each other—until eventually they've created one long train.

As the trains move, you call out various directions intended to vary the movement. Those directions can include the following:

You're going up a steep, steep hill
You're coming down the other side
You're stopping to pick up passengers
Back up
Gradually increase speed

Transportation Topics

Background Information.   This activity covers a wide variety of people and things related to transportation, some of which have not been covered by other activities. Talk about them with the children, making sure all of the images are clear.

Activity.   Ask the children to pretend to be the following:

A train engineer
The doors on a bus
A race car driver
The hood of a car
The driver of an 18-wheeler
A train whistle
Bicycle spokes

Tricycle handlebars
A blinking traffic light
The ice cream truck
The wheels on a train
A railroad gate
Railroad tracks

chapter 10
FUN THEMES

shapes
colors
the circus

SHAPES

LEARNING OBJECTIVES: To enhance bodily and spatial awareness; to offer experience with the element of shape; to stimulate visual awareness; to call attention to geometric, letter, and number shapes.

Exploring Shapes

Background Information.   Sit with the children and ask them to look around the room, making note of the different shapes of the various objects there. Can they point out something that's round? Flat? Wide?

Continue in this manner, covering (and discussing, if necessary) all the shapes listed here. Then select items in the room not yet pointed out, and ask the children to tell you what shapes they are.

Activity.   Ask the children to show you, with their bodies, the following shapes:

Round	Pointed
Flat	Crooked
Wide	Angular
Narrow	Long

Now ask them to create with their bodies the shapes of objects in the room. Possibilities include these:

A desk	The blackboard
A chair	A book
A pencil	A ruler
The globe	

Alternate Activity.   Combining shapes can make this activity much more challenging. For example, you can ask the children, alone or with partners, to create a shape that's both long and pointed, flat and round (like a pancake), or wide and angular.

Imagining Shapes

Background Information.   The previous activity requires the children to physically imitate what their eyes are seeing. With this activity, they'll be asked to use their "mind's eye." In other words, they'll have to imagine how certain things look (things that they're familiar with but are not right there in front of them) and then create the appropriate shapes with their bodies.

Listed are objects typically found in the home, since they're likely to be familiar to the children. But you should feel free to contribute ideas of your own. Just be sure to talk with the children about the things you're going to ask them to create.

Activity. Possible shapes to explore include the following:

A refrigerator

A water faucet

A dining room table

A couch

A teapot

A lamp

A telephone

A pillow

A rug

Changing Shapes

Background Information. If the children have experienced the previous activities dealing with shape, then they know that their bodies can assume a wide variety of shapes. Simply reinforce that fact and further explain that bodies can create different shapes not only while remaining in one spot, but also while moving around.

Activity. Choose a piece of music with a steady 4/4 beat that lends itself easily to walking. Instruct the children to walk about the room while the music is playing, explaining that you'll be asking them to change their bodies' shapes *as they walk*. You do this simply by calling out the shape you want them to assume. (Give them enough time to experience one shape before calling out another.) Possibilities, in addition to shapes already explored, include these:

Big

Small

Skinny

Tall

Lopsided

"Funny"

Alphabet Shapes

Background Information. Review the letters of the alphabet with the children, pointing them out on a chart or writing them on the board. Point out that some letters are made of straight and zigzagging lines, some of curved lines, and some of both. The children may choose to form either upper- or lowercase letters.

Activity. Choose letters that can be easily formed by the body, and ask the children to form them. Possibilities include I, O, T, C, X, Y, L, Q, S, U, and V.

Alternate Activities. You can also ask the children to take partners and to form letters in pairs. Here possibilities include T, X, Y, J, Q, V, W, Z, A, D, P, R, H, J, K, N, and M.

A second alternative, if your children are experienced enough, is to have groups of children create short *words* with their bodies, for instance, S-O, H-I, or L-I-P.

Finally, you can ask the children, alone or with partners, to form the shapes of numbers, too.

"Geometric Shapes"

Background Information.   Using pictures or actual objects as examples, discuss basic geometric shapes with the children. Include circles, triangles, squares, and rectangles. Ask the children to tell you how these shapes differ.

Activity.   Have the children separate into groups of three. Then, as you sing each of the following verses (to the tune of "I'm a Little Teapot"), each group forms the appropriate geometric shape.

I'm a little circle,
Round as can be.
My lines are curving—
Look at me!

I am a triangle
With three sides;
I can be narrow
Or I can be wide!

Now it's a square
That you will see.
It takes four sides
For a square to be!

Look at the rectangle—
Four sides, too.
I can change my
Shape just for you!

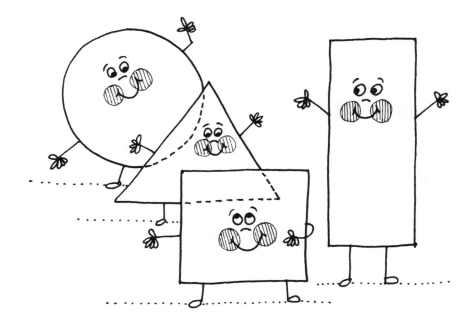

COLORS

LEARNING OBJECTIVES: To focus attention on the colors in our lives and to enhance appreciation for them.

How Deep Is the Ocean, How High Is the Sky?

Background Information. Ask the children what things they think of when you mention the color blue. Chances are their list will include water and the sky. (At least, those are the first two things that pop into *my* mind!) Talk about the different shades of blue they've seen in the ocean or the sky. Then ask them to tell you how deep they think the ocean is and how high the sky.

This activity not only calls attention to the color blue but also deals with the concepts of *high*, *middle*, and *low* as well as *up* and *down*.

Activity. Now ask the children to *show* you how deep the ocean is and how high the sky. How much distance is there between the bottom of the ocean and the sky? Where, in relation to the ocean's bottom and the sky, would they place the ocean's surface? Can they show you with their bodies?

Explain that you're going to be calling out three words—*bottom*, *surface*, and *sky*—and that when they hear one of those words, they're to show you with their bodies where the bottom, surface, and sky are in relation to one another. (If necessary, you can get more explicit, talking in terms of low, middle, and high.)

Begin calling out these words, in any order, at a slow tempo. As the children catch on, start picking up the tempo until it's as frenzied as you want it to get. Then slow it down again.

<u>Note</u>. You can also mix the tempos, keeping the children unprepared for what's going to happen next. For example, you might move quickly from bottom to surface and then very slowly to sky. In addition, you can mix up the order in which you say the words, sometimes skipping one and sometimes repeating the same one.

Mellow Yellow

Background Information. Yellow is a reminder of many pleasant things: flowers, the sun, butter, bananas, and lemon sherbet, to name a few.

What do your children think of when you mention the color yellow? Talk about the examples they cite, including the shape of each.

Activity. Ask the children to show you the *shape* of each of the following yellow things.

The sun
A lemon
A school bus
A banana

A dandelion

A diamond-shaped road sign

A pat of butter; a stick of butter; a tub of butter

Now ask them to pretend to *be* the following yellow things:

A bumblebee

A blinking yellow traffic light

A school bus

The sun shining

A lemon being squeezed

A sunflower swaying in the breeze

Butter being spread

It's Not Easy Being Green

Background Information. So sings Kermit the Frog. His point is that so many things in nature are green, he doesn't stand out. Ask the children to name some things that are green, and talk about each. Then explain that when Kermit starts this famous song, he's wishing he were a different color. But by the end of the song he's realized that green is a wonderful color to be.

Activity. Ask the children to stand in a circle, with a bit of space between them. You then move around the outside of the circle, touching each child and assigning her or him to be something green (use some of the examples cited by the children during your discussion or the possibilities listed here). One child you assign to be "frog" (or "Kermit"). You and the child then trade places. You assume the shape of a frog at your place within the circle, and the child *moves* like a frog around the circle, making the "assignments." When he or she selects another child to be a frog, they also change places. The game continues until all in the circle have been turned into frogs.

Possible green things include the following:

A leaf   A head of lettuce

A blade of grass   A pine tree

A pickle

Alternate Activity. This activity can point out just how wrong Kermit was when he thought a frog couldn't be noticed among all the other green things in nature.

Place scraps of paper, on which you've written the names of green things (see above), into a container. Put in only one scrap of paper with the word *frog* on it.

Choose one child to be the "guesser." That child then either leaves the room or stands aside, with eyes or ears covered, while the rest of the children draw papers. These children then quickly take on the shapes they've drawn. When they're ready, you let the guesser know. She or he then tries to identify which child is the "frog," with the object being to do so as quickly as possible. Once identified, the frog becomes the guesser, and the game continues.

Hot and Cold Colors

Background Information.   Ask the children what the color red makes them *feel*. Does it bring heat to mind? What about the color blue? Does that make them think of the cold? Discuss some of the reasons why red and blue bring hot and cold to mind. For example, flames (and fire trucks) are mostly red. And blue is the color that lips can turn when someone's been in the cold too long—for instance, in the cold blue ocean.

Activity.   Ask the children to pretend to be the following:

> Red-hot barbecue coals
> Ocean waves
> A sizzling fire
> A blue popsicle

Now ask them to show you how the following make their bodies *react*.

> Running into the cold ocean
> Touching a red-hot stove
> Jumping into a cold swimming pool
> Walking under a red-hot sun
> Being out in the cold too long

Primary Colors

Background Information.   *Primary colors* are defined by *Webster's Third New International Dictionary* as "any of a set of colors from which all other colors may be derived." Traditionally, the primary colors with which we work are red, yellow, and blue. Red and yellow combine to make orange. Yellow and blue combine to make green. And red and blue combine to give us purple.

Talk to the children about primary colors and their combinations. Or, better still, *show* them—with crayons or paints or pictures in a book.

Activity.   Divide your class into three groups and assign each group a primary color. Ask each group (either in turn or all at the same time) to pretend to be as many different things in their color as they can think of. They can perform these examples either individually or with other members of the group. If they need help, you can offer suggestions. For the yellow group, suggest those things listed in Mellow Yellow. For red and blue, possibilities include the following:

Red	Blue
An apple	The ocean
A fire engine	The sky
A strawberry	A bluebird
Hot coals	A blueberry
The planet Mars	The blue lines on notebook paper
A rose	A police officer's uniform
A heart	The flashing light on a police car

Now assign one child from each group to pair up with a child from a different group. Each pair must then depict something in the color they've created with their joining. For example, if a child from the red group and a child from the blue group pair up, they should create something purple. You can ask one pair at a time to do this (demonstrating for the rest of the class) or you can ask all of the pairs to work simultaneously.

If the children need help, you can offer suggestions. Possibilities for green can be found under It's Not Easy Being Green. Possibilities for orange and purple follow:

Orange	*Purple*
An orange	A grape or bunch of grapes
A ladybug	A plum
A monarch butterfly	An eggplant
A carrot	A pansy
Orange juice	Lilacs

THE CIRCUS

LEARNING OBJECTIVES: To stimulate the imagination; to have an excuse to move; to have fun!

The Tightrope Walker

Background Information. After clowns, one of the most common images of the circus is the tightrope, also known as the high wire. That one piece of rope or wire is the focus of quite a lot of excitement under the "big top."

Have any of your children ever seen a tightrope act? How do they think a tightrope walker gets from one side to the other without falling off? Balance is the key! What do the children think it means to have good balance?

Activity. Create a "tightrope" on the floor with chalk or masking tape (unless you already have a straight line running across the floor to serve the purpose). Then tell the children to pretend to be tightrope walkers making their way across the high wire. (You may want to assure them there's a net below!)

Once each child has crossed successfully, challenge her or him to try it sideways and then backward. Are there any other ways they can move across the tightrope without stepping off?

Everybody Loves a Clown

Background Information. Probably nobody loves a clown more than a child—because children love to laugh. Clowns come in all shapes and sizes, of course (just like regular people), but there are some things you can pretty much count on with all clowns. Can the children tell you what those things are?

Activity. Ask the children to each pretend to be a circus clown doing the following:

Walking around in big floppy shoes
Honking her or his red nose
Juggling
Riding a unicycle
Riding a unicycle and juggling at the same time
Jumping on the trampoline (sometimes high; sometimes low)
Entertaining the audience

Note. The last suggestion is wide open to individual interpretation, giving the children a chance to "clown" in any way they want.

Elephants, Tigers, and Seals—Oh My!

Background Information.   Among the most commonly seen animals in circuses—besides the trained horses—are elephants, tigers, and seals. The elephants circle the ring, walking on hind legs or carrying clowns or ladies dressed in tutus. The tigers jump through hoops or allow the trainer to put his or her head into their mouths. And the seals clap their fins together and play bicycle horns with their mouths. What else do the children think these circus animals might do?

Activity.   Ask the children to form a circle—just like a ring in the circus. Acting as ring-master, you stand in the center. Pointing at one child at a time, you call out either *elephant*, *tiger*, or *seal*. That child then performs a "trick" that that particular animal might be seen performing at the circus. Continue until every child has had a chance to be at least one animal.

Alternate Activity.   To make a grand exit, the children can walk around in the circle chanting "Elephants, tigers, and seals—oh my!" and making accompanying movements, which you've prearranged. For example, the word *elephant* might inspire a "trunk" being raised and lowered. *Tiger* might call for "whiskers" or pointed "ears" made with the fingers. Two hand claps with outstretched arms might be just the movement for *seal*. And *oh my!* could be accompanied by the palms of the hands coming to the sides of the face, with mouth and eyes wide open. Once the children have repeated the chant a few times, you can step in front of one of the children and lead a parade of circus performers out in style (out the door or back to their desks, for instance) to the imagined roar of the crowd.

"Stiltwalker"

Background Information.   Have the children ever seen anybody walk on stilts? Describe it as best you can or, if possible, show the children a picture. What do they think it would be like to walk on such tall sticks—to be up so high? Talk about the sensations and images mentioned in the following poem.

Activity.   Ask the children to pretend to be stiltwalkers at the circus as they act out this poem. The last two lines lend themselves to exploration. What kinds of "tricks" do they think could be performed on stilts? The poem is as follows:

> Up so high upon my stilts,
> The ground so far below;
> I can sway and I can tilt,
> But I won't fall, you know.
>
> It takes time, but I can turn
> With lots of little steps.
> There's no need to be concerned—
> I've got a lot of pep.

With giant steps I can go
Around the circus grounds,
Saying hi to those I know,
The acrobats and clowns.

And at the end of a day
Of walking on two sticks,
It is time for me to play
With learning some new tricks!

"Ringmaster"

Background Information.   Technically, the ringmaster is the person in charge of the performance of the trained horses. But he or she can take on other duties as well. And no matter what he or she is doing, the center of the ring is usually where it's being done.

Review all of the circus activities already explored, and talk about any others you and the children can think of (for instance, the trained horses and trapeze artists).

Activity.   This is a variation on a game called Punchinello, with which you and the children may already be familiar. In that game, one child ("Punchinello") stands in the center of the circle with the others all around. The other children then chant a rhyme that asks Punchinello what she or he can do. Punchinello shows them; they proclaim in rhyme that they can do it, too; and then they do.

This activity is the same, except the child in the center will be called "Ringmaster," so the rhyme must also change. And the movement the child in the center performs must be something that could be seen at a circus. A new ringmaster then enters the ring, and the chant is repeated.

The chant is as follows:

> What can you do, Ringmaster, Ringmaster?
> What can you do, Ringmaster, you?
>
> (The child in center demonstrates an action.)
>
> We can do it, too, Ringmaster, Ringmaster.
> We can do it, too, Ringmaster, you!
>
> (And they do!)

ABOUT THE AUTHOR

While teaching dance to young children in 1979, Rae Pica realized that the children didn't need technique as much as they needed the opportunity to express themselves through movement. A year later, Rae was hiring and training instructors and sending them to local day-care centers and preschools, and a company called Moving & Learning was born.

Since that time, Rae, a movement education specialist, and her husband, Richard Gardzina, a musician and composer, have created the Moving & Learning Series for early childhood and elementary professionals, combining tailor-made music with developmentally appropriate movement activities.

The author, lyricist, and vocalist for this unique series, Rae has conducted movement workshops for such groups as the National Association for the Education of Young Children, the American Montessori Society and the National Center for Montessori Education, the United States Gymnastics Federation, the Association for Childhood Education International, and state, district, and national levels of the American Alliance for Health, Physical Education, Recreation and Dance. (For information about sponsoring a movement workshop for your school, center, or organization, call Rae at 603-332-6917.)

Rae has written widely on the subject of movement, music, and dance, with articles appearing in *Instructor Magazine, Preschool Perspectives, Early Childhood Music,* and *International Gymnast.* She is the author of *Toddlers Moving & Learning, Let's Move & Learn, Special Themes for Moving & Learning, Poetry in Motion: Poems & Activities for Moving & Learning with Young Children* and *Dance Training for Gymnastics.* Rae is the host of ''Move for a Minute,'' initially produced by New Hampshire Public Television in 1984 and later broadcast nationwide on public television. In addition, she teaches movement fundamentals and elementary physical education pedagogy to physical education majors at the University of New Hampshire. Rae serves on the editorial board of the newsletter *Teaching Elementary Physical Education* and is coauthor of the *YMCA Preschool Movement and Health Program.*